Face to the Rising Sun

Reflections on Spirituals and Justice

D1516387

Mark Francisco Bozzuti-Jones

Face to the Rising Sun

Reflections on Spirituals and Justice

Mark Francisco Bozzuti-Jones

FORWARD MOVEMENT
Cincinnati, Ohio

Library of Congress Cataloging-in-Publication Data

Names: Bozzuti-Jones, Mark Francisco, 1966- author.
Title: Face to the rising sun : reflections on spirituals and justice /
  Mark Francisco Bozzuti-Jones.
Description: Cincinnati, Ohio : Forward Movement, [2021] | Summary:
  "Spirituals, songs of abiding faith passed down by African Americans
  through the centuries, offer a remarkable view of resilience, courage,
  and love. Formed in the crucible of fire, these songs express the
  suffering and horror of slavery as well as the love of God and the
  promise of a better future. Author Mark Bozzuti-Jones explores the
  modern-day lessons of these Spirituals with scripture readings, daily
  devotions, and questions for reflection. With 31 days of devotions, Face
  to the Rising Sun offers a path forward, a way to repent and name the
  evils of racism and to learn and grow together in God's love"-- Provided
  by publisher.
Identifiers: LCCN 2021019939 (print) | LCCN 2021019940 (ebook) | ISBN
  9780880284998 | ISBN 9780880284998 (ebook)
Subjects: LCSH: Spirituals (Songs)--Devotional use. | Social
  justice--Prayers and devotions.
Classification: LCC ML3556 .B69 2021 (print) | LCC ML3556 (ebook) | DDC
  782.25/3--dc23
LC record available at https://lccn.loc.gov/2021019939
LC ebook record available at https://lccn.loc.gov/2021019940

Forward
Movement
inspire disciples. empower evangelists

Dedicated to Mark Anthony Francisco
and the Rev. Dr. Kathy Bozzuti-Jones

And to my mother,
Muriel Jestina Townsend,
who sang all these Spirituals to me

TABLE OF CONTENTS

INTRODUCTION

The words of these Spirituals resound through the centuries. Like the crucified Jesus on the cross, one can hear the Slaves crying out through the centuries the very words of Jesus on the cross: "My God, my God, why have you forsaken me?" We hear Slaves demonstrate the cost of discipleship and a commitment to their faith in God "when people revile you and persecute you and utter all kinds of evil against you" (Matthew 5:12).

In the sacrament of Holy Eucharist as we share in the Body and Blood of Christ, we always say words akin to these: "do this in memory of me." To sing Spirituals is to sing in memory of the Slaves and their faith, to recall these songs sung for centuries and handed down to us today as part of the legacy of the African American culture.

In the Christian tradition, prayer and remembering are always a call to action, always a call to repentance, and always a call to redemptive living. When we sing the Spirituals today, we commit to living a life of prayer that ensures justice for all, a life that calls us to make amends for the evil of slavery, and a life that calls us to work against the forces of racism and discrimination still present in our societies today.

The words of these Spirituals offer a more revolutionary, prophetic, and radical view of Slaves' faith than is often acknowledged. In truth, the Spirituals are credal statements uttered in the crucible of fire. Like the crucified Jesus on the cross, the Slaves through these Spirituals revealed the cruelty, horror, and sin of those who enslaved and crucified them. Slavery represents the crucifixion of the Slaves from Africa and their unwavering faith in God who did not abandon them. Tradition has it that Jesus uttered seven "words" on the cross; in the Spirituals we see the "seven words" of all the Slaves.

At the same time, the Spirituals express a deep and abiding faith, an understanding by Slaves that they were beloved children of

God, made in God's image. Unwilling to accept the limitations set by the slave masters, Slaves used song to express the love of God and God's desire for their freedom. Spirituals became code for sharing hope and the promise of a better future.

We hear this longing in the words of the Spiritual, "Let Us Break Bread Together." The Spiritual offers an image of equality as we come to the Lord's Table together, as one body, with our "face to the rising sun."

The Spirituals sung by Slaves have much to teach us today as we seek justice and a society of equality, freedom, and respect. The Spirituals arose in a time when Black lives did not matter, and their words echo on in the chants and protests today through the Black Lives Matter movement.

This movement calls our attention to the repeated killing of African Americans by police throughout the United States. Trayvon Martin, Eric Garner, Michael Brown, Tanisha Anderson, Tamir Rice, Walter Scott, Breonna Taylor, and George Floyd are just some of the names of those killed by police, oftentimes with no accountability. The Black Lives Matter movement insists we must work together, with urgency, for justice and equality, on our streets and in our schools, in our communities and our churches, and throughout our public lives.

These daily devotions, steeped in scripture and covered by prayer, ask us to examine the Spirituals as a way for us to learn and grow together. In pastoral letters, the Episcopal Church has called racism a "pervasive sin" and firmly and decidedly expressed its condemnation of slavery, racism, and all the effects that flow from these two realities. As a nation, as churches, and as people of faith, we are tasked with repentance in the area of racism.

Together we must face the sin and harm done to the Slaves and the hurt and pain that continue to impact the lives of African Americans because of systemic racism. The Episcopal Church, the Roman Catholic Church, and many Christian and non-

Christian religious groups have pledged to shed light on racism, name it, confront it, challenge it, and make amends for all the harm that slavery has caused, and racism continues to do.

As Christians, we seek forgiveness, make amends, and commit to social justice, change, and peace through and in our prayers. *Face to the Rising Sun* encourages the reader to put faith into action. For too long, many have believed that prayer is a passive activity. Now more than ever, we recognize the importance of practicing what we preach as we try to live in such a way to respect the dignity of every human being.

These Spirituals can serve as part of a covenant that we enter into with one another to stand up for justice and peace, eradicate racism, seek justice and peace, practice reconciliation, and give voice to words that further announce the reign of God's love. In truth, we are called to live and sing these Spirituals and our own Spirituals for today.

HOW TO USE THIS BOOK

These thirty-one meditations can be used daily throughout a month or over a longer period of time. One may use the book privately, with a spiritual director, or in a small group for prayerful conversation.

Read and/or Sing the Spiritual

Each day's meditation has a Spiritual. Read or sing the Spiritual. If you're unfamiliar with the tune or melody, search for it online. You can also visit forwardmovement.org/risingsun, which includes a playlist with the Spirituals. I chose the most common lyrics for the Spirituals, but as with songs handed down over the centuries, the words may be different in your memory. Sing them as you learned them, for they are prayers of the heart.

Each day, spend some time with the Spiritual. See how the Spiritual might be calling you to deepen your love of God and your commitment to respect the dignity of every human being.

There are three questions you could ask yourself independently of the questions provided:

- What does the Spiritual say about the experience of the Slaves?

- How might the Spiritual be calling you to learn something new about slavery and racism in America?

- How is the Spiritual inviting you to put your faith in action?

Read the Scriptures

How we read and interpret the Bible matters. We call the Bible the Word of God; however, it is how we live these words that demonstrate if they are the Word of God. For the Bible to truly be the word of God, there is a mandatory requirement of love. We must love God and love our neighbor as ourselves. Slavery demonstrated a misreading of the Bible and a deliberate denial of biblical truths. Slavery stands as a reminder that the Christian community can remain deaf to the call of God, obstinate to the call of love, and contrary to the desires of God even while reading the Bible and claiming it as the Word of God.

Today, as we read the scriptures, we hope that our thoughts, words, and actions are more aligned with the Way of Love, God's call for us to love and respect each other. Reading the scriptures today invites us to a self-examination of our present reality and history. To read the scriptures today is to think about what our spiritual ancestors and spiritual contemporaries got wrong and continue to get wrong. How is it that we read the scriptures and fail to go in peace, to love and serve the Lord, and to be examples of God's love? Today when we read the Bible, we always have to ask ourselves if we are reading it with the heart and eyes of God.

How does our reading of the scriptures today lead us to justice, reconciliation, and truth?

The scriptures in this devotional book are chosen to help us think about our reaction to slavery and how we are called to love our neighbor and respect the dignity of every human being today. Indeed, the hope is that when we read the scriptures, we read them with a repentant heart and renewed commitment to God's light, love, and truth.

Ask yourself:

- How do these Bible passages call you to pay attention to justice and peace for all?

- What do these passages have to teach you about how to be God's presence in the world today?

- How do these passages call you to repentance and commitment to respect the dignity of every human being?

Read the Poems

Throughout the book, I included a number of poems I wrote that treat present-day issues of social injustice and the experience of racism in America today. I invite you to read them a few times, at any one sitting, and enter into dialogue with them, in a prayerful spirit. Notice how God speaks to you through them. Notice what emotions they evoke in you. They offer an opportunity for journaling, art response, and conversation. Here are some ways to engage with the poems prayerfully:

- Where do you find the voice of God in these poems?

- How do they relate to a question or struggle in your spiritual life?

- Is there an affirmation or insight among them that moves you to take action?

Spiritual Reflection and Commitment

The life of prayer is all about reflection and commitment. We pray daily in order to surrender ourselves to God's will and to commit to being messengers of good news in the world. As we respond to the ills of systemic racism, our prayers must lead to reflection, repentance, and commitment to living the good news.

For this section of the daily meditation, the invitation is to open your mind, heart, and soul to what is being shared. See how the reflection calls you to a deeper understanding of the Spirituals, the experience of slavery, and a commitment to live a life that acknowledges the painful reality of slavery, ongoing racism, and a call to walk in the way of love.

* * *

The devotions are designed to provide a month of daily readings and reflection at any time of year. But my prayer is that this is not a book read once and discarded or put on a shelf to gather dust. I invite you to read and reread it, just as we do with scripture, making it a spiritual companion, finding new messages and deeper meaning with each reading. Moreover, this book can be a spirit-filled guide for a group study and prayer companion during the various liturgical seasons.

Let us not just sing the Spirituals but live the Spirituals.

May God bless and keep you always. May every day with the Spirituals be sweeter than the day before.

Those Knees

You have your knees on our lives
knees on our head
knees on our neck
knees on our chest
knees on our belly
knees on our groin
knees on our, those, private parts
knees on our backside
knees on our legs
knees on our feet
knees on our hands
knees on our flesh
knees on our bone
We can't breathe
We can't breathe (Lord, have mercy)
We can't breathe (Mama)
We can't breathe (Help)
We can't breathe (God, help me)
We can't breathe (Please)
We can't breathe (Stop)
We can't breathe—gasp, gasp, gasp, gasp
We won't take it anymore
We want to live
Even with our dying breath, we know,
you cannot kneel on our soul
We will live. Remove your knees.

Nobody Knows the Troubles I've Seen

Nobody knows the troubles I've seen.
Nobody knows but Jesus.
Nobody knows the trouble I've seen.
Glory, Alleluia.

Sometimes, I'm up.
Sometimes, I'm down (oh, yes, Lord).
Sometimes, I'm almost
To the ground (oh, yes, Lord).

Nobody knows the troubles I've seen.
Nobody knows but Jesus.
Nobody knows the trouble I've seen.
Glory, Alleluia.

If you get there before I do (oh, yes, Lord),
Tell all my friends, I'm coming too (oh, yes, Lord).
Nobody knows the troubles I've seen.
Nobody knows but Jesus.
Nobody knows the trouble I've seen.
Glory, Alleluia.

SCRIPTURE
Genesis 37:12-28

Now his brothers went to pasture their father's flock near Shechem. And Israel said to Joseph, "Are not your brothers pasturing the flock at Shechem? Come, I will send you to them." He answered, "Here I am." So he said to him, "Go now, see if it is well with your brothers and with the flock; and bring word back to me." So he sent him from the valley of Hebron. He came to Shechem, and a man found him wandering in the fields; the man asked him, "What are you seeking?" "I am seeking my brothers," he said; "tell me, please, where they are pasturing the flock." The man said, "They have gone away, for I heard them say, 'Let us go to Dothan.'" So Joseph went after his brothers, and found them at Dothan. They saw him from a distance, and before he came near to them, they conspired to kill him. They said to one another, "Here comes this dreamer. Come now, let us kill him and throw him into one of the pits; then we shall say that a wild animal has devoured him, and we shall see what will become of his dreams." But when Reuben heard it, he delivered him out of their hands, saying, "Let us not take his life." Reuben said to them, "Shed no blood; throw him into this pit here in the wilderness, but lay no hand on him"—that he might rescue him out of their hand and restore him to his father.

So when Joseph came to his brothers, they stripped him of his robe, the long robe with sleeves that he wore; and they took him and threw him into a pit. The pit was empty; there was no water in it. Then they sat down to eat; and looking up they saw a caravan of Ishmaelites coming from Gilead, with their camels carrying gum, balm, and resin, on their way to carry it down to Egypt. Then Judah said to his brothers, "What profit is it if we kill our brother and conceal his blood? Come, let us sell him to the Ishmaelites, and not lay our hands on him, for he is our brother, our own flesh." And his brothers agreed. When some Midianite traders passed by, they drew Joseph up, lifting him out of the pit, and sold him to the Ishmaelites for twenty pieces of silver. And they took Joseph to Egypt.

Psalm 1:1-3

Happy are they who have not walked in the counsel of the wicked, nor lingered in the way of sinners, nor sat in the seats of the scornful! Their delight is in the law of the LORD, and they meditate on his law day and night. They are like trees planted by streams of water, bearing fruit in due season, with leaves that do not wither; everything they do shall prosper.

Luke 10:25-37

Just then a lawyer stood up to test Jesus. "Teacher," he said, "what must I do to inherit eternal life?" He said to him, "What is written in the law? What do you read there?" He answered, "You shall love the Lord your God with all your heart, and with all your soul, and with all your strength, and with all your mind; and your neighbor as yourself." And he said to him, "You have given the right answer; do this, and you will live." But wanting to justify himself, he asked Jesus, "And who is my neighbor?" Jesus replied, "A man was going down from Jerusalem to Jericho, and fell into the hands of robbers, who stripped him, beat him, and went away, leaving him half dead. Now by chance a priest was going down that road; and when he saw him, he passed by on the other side. So likewise a Levite, when he came to the place and saw him, passed by on the other side. But a Samaritan while traveling came near him; and when he saw him, he was moved with pity. He went to him and bandaged his wounds, having poured oil and wine on them. Then he put him on his own animal, brought him to an inn, and took care of him. The next day he took out two denarii, gave them to the innkeeper, and said, 'Take care of him; and when I come back, I will repay you whatever more you spend.' Which of these three, do you think, was a neighbor to the man who fell into the hands of the robbers?" He said, "The one who showed him mercy." Jesus said to him, "Go and do likewise."

SPIRITUAL REFLECTION

"Nobody Knows the Troubles I've Seen" is one of the most haunting of Spirituals. *Nobody knows the troubles I've seen.* As a child, I thought the line went like this: "Nobody knows the troubles I feel." Seen or felt, there are many troubles for African Americans in the United States. From the time most of their ancestors arrived as Slaves over four hundred years ago to the present, African Americans have felt and seen too many troubles.

African American history has been marked by troubles from slavery, through periods of segregation, the fight for civil rights, and present-day racism and discrimination. We have seen troubles—the unimaginable and painful troubles of slavery's legacy. The Slaves sang of their troubles—the dehumanizing treatments meted out to them. They had to fight for their freedom and struggle to assert their humanity.

That the cries of the Slaves have been called Spirituals is a lesson in itself. There is no denying that the Slaves from Africa came with their own spiritual lives. African history, anthropology, and religious studies point to a deep commitment and awareness of the "spirit." Slaves were spiritual beings and spiritually aware.

Our gospel reading reminds us to notice the behavior of the good Samaritan. Note how the Samaritan responds to the suffering of the person who was robbed and nearly beaten to death, while the legal and religious experts of the day ignored his suffering. Now more than ever, the church, the country, and all spiritual people are called to attend to those who have been robbed and wounded along the paths of life. African Americans and all who support justice and equality urge us to respond to those most in need of mercy in our society.

It is no small wonder that the Slaves identified easily with the suffering of Jesus. They saw in his agony, sorrow, and suffering something akin to what they were going through. What they heard about Jesus and what they learned about his suffering and the cross convinced them that Jesus understood the unjust suffering they endured. Nobody knows but Jesus.

SPIRITUAL COMMITMENT

- Reread the Spiritual. How might God be calling you to know more about the past and present troubles of African Americans?

- Spend some time reading Dr. Martin Luther King Jr.'s "Letter from a Birmingham Jail" or the book, *The Autobiography of Malcolm X: As Told to Alex Haley.*

- The psalm appointed for today speaks about crying out from the depths. Hear yourself read it aloud. Pray for the grace to listen more deeply to the African American experience.

- How is God calling you to be a good Samaritan?

- What do these scriptures have to teach us about a Christian response to the reality of African Americans?

Go Down, Moses

When Israel was in Egypt's land,
Let my people go.
Oppressed so hard they could not stand,
Let my people go.

Refrain:
Go down, Moses,
Way down in Egypt's land.
Tell old Pharaoh,
Let my people go.

SCRIPTURE
Exodus 3:1-12

Moses was keeping the flock of his father-in-law Jethro, the priest of Midian; he led his flock beyond the wilderness, and came to Horeb, the mountain of God. There the angel of the LORD appeared to him in a flame of fire out of a bush; he looked, and the bush was blazing, yet it was not consumed. Then Moses said, "I must turn aside and look at this great sight, and see why the bush is not burned up." When the LORD saw that he had turned aside to see, God called to him out of the bush, "Moses, Moses!" And he said, "Here I am." Then he said, "Come no closer! Remove the sandals from your feet, for the place on which you are standing is holy ground." He said further, "I am the God of your father, the God of Abraham, the God of Isaac, and the God of Jacob." And Moses hid his face, for he was afraid to look at God.

Then the LORD said, "I have observed the misery of my people who are in Egypt; I have heard their cry on account of their taskmasters. Indeed, I know their sufferings, and I have come down to deliver them from the Egyptians, and to bring them up out of that land to a good and broad land, a land flowing with milk and honey, to the country of the Canaanites, the Hittites, the Amorites, the Perizzites, the Hivites, and the Jebusites. The cry of the Israelites has now come to me; I have also seen how the Egyptians oppress them. So come, I will send you to Pharaoh to bring my people, the Israelites, out of Egypt."

But Moses said to God, "Who am I that I should go to Pharaoh, and bring the Israelites out of Egypt?" He said, "I will be with you; and this shall be the sign for you that it is I who sent you: when you have brought the people out of Egypt, you shall worship God on this mountain."

Psalm 5:1-3

Give ear to my words, O Lord; consider my meditation. Hearken to my cry for help, my King and my God, for I make my prayer to you. In the morning, LORD, you hear my voice; early in the morning I make my appeal and watch for you.

Luke 10:25-28

Just then a lawyer stood up to test Jesus. "Teacher," he said, "what must I do to inherit eternal life?" He said to him, "What is written in the law? What do you read there?" He answered, "You shall love the Lord your God with all your heart, and with all your soul, and with all your strength, and with all your mind; and your neighbor as yourself." And he said to him, "You have given the right answer; do this, and you will live."

SPIRITUAL REFLECTION

"Go Down, Moses" is one of the best-known Spirituals. It has tremendous relevance for our country today, because we need a new Moses. Truth be told, we need a band of prophets like Moses. African Americans live in a society where their rights are ignored and where systemic racism prevents them from having access to health care, meaningful work, safe housing, and proper educational opportunities. The story of Moses delivering the people of Israel out of Egypt and freeing them from slavery assured the Slaves that God would also deliver them.

How do we live the call to love God and neighbor in response to these injustices? Jesus has commanded it. The call to love is required of us and is as urgent today as ever. To love our neighbors is to love God; love of God is expressed in justice, not in racism or discrimination. The God we meet in Jesus Christ is a God who reminds us to love our neighbors as we love ourselves.

Love is expressed in liberating justice. African Americans seek to be liberated from the effects of racism that cause them to die before their time, often dying at the hands of the very police who should protect them.

Black Lives Matter. Black Lives Matter. Black Lives Matter. If we know anything about God, it is that those who are most in need and most oppressed matter to God. In the United States of America today, our Black and Brown brothers and sisters are murdered at a higher rate and in more brutal ways by the police than any other group.

The Black Lives Matter movement began in response to continued killing of Black men and women by the police. Oftentimes, these police officers have been acquitted, leaving the Black families and the wider population to wonder: Where is the justice for the Black population in the United States? On May 25, 2020, George Floyd was killed, as an arresting police office kneeled on his neck for nine minutes and thirty seconds. Floyd cried out for his mother and screamed that he could not breathe. This did not move the policeman or prompt four of his colleagues to come to Floyd's aid. Instead, Floyd died with a knee on his neck. The whole incident was captured on video. His death reminded America of a similar cry from Eric Garner, who died on July 17, 2014, on Staten Island, who screamed the same words before he died from a policeman's chokehold, "I can't breathe."

Our Christian call is one in which we must participate in the liberation of all peoples; we must ensure that all of us can breathe. The words from the Spiritual, "oppressed so hard they could not stand. Let my people go," remind us of the call to be agents of liberation.

SPIRITUAL COMMITMENT

- Reread the Spiritual. How might God be sending you out to be part of the liberation of African Americans?

- What do the words, "I can't breathe" stir up in your soul?

- What do you believe the deaths of Eric Garner and George Floyd have to teach us about being a just society?

- What do these scriptures have to teach us about a Christian response to Black Lives Matter?

- How do you think God might be calling you to "Let my people go?"

Were You There When They Crucified My Lord?

Were you there when they crucified my Lord?
Were you there when they crucified my Lord?
Sometimes it causes me to tremble, tremble, tremble.
Were you there when they crucified my Lord?

Were you there when you nailed him to the tree?
Were you there when you nailed him to the tree?
Sometimes it causes me to tremble, tremble, tremble.
Were you there when you nailed him to the tree?

Were you there when they laid him in the tomb?
Were you there when they laid him in the tomb?
Sometimes it causes me to tremble, tremble, tremble.
Were you there when they laid him in the tomb?

SCRIPTURE
Numbers 11:10-15

Moses heard the people weeping throughout their families, all at the entrances of their tents. Then the LORD became very angry, and Moses was displeased. So Moses said to the LORD, "Why have you treated your servant so badly? Why have I not found favor in your sight, that you lay the burden of all this people on me? Did I conceive all this people? Did I give birth to them, that you should say to me, 'Carry them in your bosom, as a nurse carries a sucking child,' to the land that you promised on oath to their ancestors? Where am I to get meat to give to all this people? For they come weeping to me and say, 'Give us meat to eat!' I am not able to carry all this people alone, for they are too heavy for me. If this is the way you are going to treat me, put me to death at once—if I have found favor in your sight—and do not let me see my misery."

Psalm 27:1-4

The LORD is my light and my salvation; whom then shall I fear? The LORD is the strength of my life; of whom then shall I be afraid?

When evildoers came upon me to eat up my flesh, it was they, my foes and my adversaries, who stumbled and fell. Though an army should encamp against me, yet my heart shall not be afraid; And though war should rise up against me, yet will I put my trust in him.

Matthew 3:1-10

In those days John the Baptist appeared in the wilderness of Judea, proclaiming, "Repent, for the kingdom of heaven has come near." This is the one of whom the prophet Isaiah spoke when he said, "The voice of one crying out in the wilderness: 'Prepare the way of the Lord, make his paths straight.'" Now John wore clothing of camel's hair with a leather belt around his waist, and his food was locusts and wild honey. Then the people of Jerusalem and all Judea were going out to him, and all the region along the Jordan, and they were baptized by him in the river Jordan, confessing their sins.

But when he saw many Pharisees and Sadducees coming for baptism, he said to them, "You brood of vipers! Who warned you to flee from the wrath to come? Bear fruit worthy of repentance. Do not presume to say to yourselves, 'We have Abraham as our ancestor'; for I tell you, God is able from these stones to raise up children to Abraham. Even now the ax is lying at the root of the trees; every tree therefore that does not bear good fruit is cut down and thrown into the fire."

SPIRITUAL REFLECTION

Oftentimes, the response to claims of Black Lives Matter is All Lives Matter. Of course, all lives matter. But this phrase is mere charade unless all of America experiences a sense that their lives really do matter enough to protect and defend and promote. In this country, racism is expressed in the killing of Black people in disproportionate numbers and inhumane ways. Black Lives Matter cries out in the wilderness of America and asks America to fulfill its commitment to the claim that all are created equal. Only then can we honestly say that all lives matter.

Were you there? The question posed in the Spiritual is often asked in another way when it comes to tragedy: Where were you? Where were you when you heard the news about George Floyd, the death of Princess Diana, 9/11 attacks, Rwandan genocide, fires in the Amazon, or the assassinations of President Kennedy and Dr. Martin Luther King Jr.? Where were you? We tend to remember and associate these events with a place.

In the Spiritual, the words "were you there?" cry out to the listener to remember suffering in a time and place that rings true in our time and place as well. Sung by the Slaves, it is first a question to their masters, referring to what they had learned about the passion of Jesus Christ. This question indicted their masters as well as the white church in their day. Were you there when this happened to Jesus? And how can you allow it, here?

It is common in African proverbs that every question spans the past, the present, and the future. So, the question of the Spiritual has three dimensions: were you there, are you there now, and will you be there? Where are the powerful, the religious leaders, the spiritual people, the rest of society, and all those who claim to love justice, mercy, and peace? Where have you been? Where are you headed? The very thought of the suffering of Jesus made the Slaves tremble. Likewise, the Spiritual asks each of us to pay attention and to examine ourselves—past, present, and future—in relation to the face of oppression, racism, and injustice.

The Black Lives Matter movement, at its truest, is about protest, not violent protest. It acts as a mirror to the Christian community, seeking to reflect the commitments of Moses and John the Baptist. John spoke truth to power, and Moses worked to liberate the people. How are we called to speak truth to power today? How are we called to liberate the people?

SPIRITUAL COMMITMENT

- Reread the Spiritual. How might God be sending you to be part of the liberation of African Americans?

- Commit to reading about John the Baptist and the depiction of Jesus's crucifixion in the gospels.

- The Black Lives Matter movement has a protest chant, "Say their names!" Why do you think this is important?

- What do these scriptures have to teach us about a Christian response to the Black Lives Matter movement?

- How is God calling you to be present to the suffering of others?

Let Us Break Bread Together

Let us break bread together on our knees.
Let us break bread together on our knees.
When I fall on my knees with my face to the rising sun,
Oh Lord, have mercy on me.

Let us drink wine together on our knees.
Let us drink wine together on our knees.
When I fall on my knees with my face to the rising sun,
Oh Lord, have mercy on me.

SCRIPTURE

Deuteronomy 4:1-8

So now, Israel, give heed to the statutes and ordinances that I am teaching you to observe, so that you may live to enter and occupy the land that the LORD, the God of your ancestors, is giving you. You must neither add anything to what I command you nor take away anything from it, but keep the commandments of the LORD your God with which I am charging you. You have seen for yourselves what the LORD did with regard to the Baal of Peor—how the LORD your God destroyed from among you everyone who followed the Baal of Peor, while those of you who held fast to the LORD your God are all alive today. See, just as the LORD my God has charged me, I now teach you statutes and ordinances for you to observe in the land that you are about to enter and occupy. You must observe them diligently, for this will show your wisdom and discernment to the peoples, who, when they hear all these statutes, will say, "Surely this great nation is a wise and discerning people!" For what other great nation has a god so near to it as the LORD our God is whenever we call to him?

And what other great nation has statutes and ordinances as just as this entire law that I am setting before you today?

Psalm 31:9-10

Have mercy on me, O Lord, for I am in trouble; my eye is consumed with sorrow, and also my throat and my belly. For my life is wasted with grief, and my years with sighing; my strength fails me because of affliction, and my bones are consumed.

Matthew 4:12-17

Now when Jesus heard that John had been arrested, he withdrew to Galilee. He left Nazareth and made his home in Capernaum by the sea, in the territory of Zebulun and Naphtali, so that what had been spoken through the prophet Isaiah might be fulfilled: "Land of Zebulun, land of Naphtali, on the road by the sea, across the Jordan, Galilee of the Gentiles—the people who sat in darkness have seen a great light, and for those who sat in the region and shadow of death light has dawned." From that time Jesus began to proclaim, "Repent, for the kingdom of heaven has come near."

SPIRITUAL REFLECTION

Anybody who has broken bread with others in good faith knows that betrayal sits at the table of fellowship. We betray each other. Jesus calls us to express our betrayals with courage, as he did when he broke bread together on his knees with his family, friends, and disciples. Our work in identifying systemic racism is all about breaking bread together and acknowledging that one of us has betrayed us. One of us is betraying us. In the spirit of Jesus, we are called to affirm that all are in need of God's mercy and justice, and so we continue to come to the table. The work is to celebrate the fellowship and supper of all, even with the betrayals, and journey, intentionally, to a place of deeper communion. Let us break bread together and let us drink wine together.

In 1964, Dr. Martin Luther King Jr. pointed out that the most segregated hour in America was Sunday during morning worship. More than five decades later, this still holds true in most communities. Through our baptismal covenant and our life as disciples of Christ, we are called to break this cycle of segregation and to respect the dignity of every human being and seek to do so in a spirit of oneness.

This Spiritual is a call to break bread together and drink wine together. Indeed, a very strong call embedded in these words is that we all seek the common good in our interaction. Part of the power of these simple words is that they call us to true worship in daily communion. The breaking of bread and the drinking of wine require that we fall on our knees together, desiring to live in communion with each other and with our God. This is expressed in the table fellowship of Holy Eucharist.

What does it mean to be together? It is said that racism is America's original sin. Racism, by its very nature, prevents us from co-existing in love. All that we read in scripture is an ongoing invitation to repent and find ways to love God and love one another in God. Racism has no place in the pursuit of togetherness. Human beings are made to live together in freedom, liberation, and justice. Christians and spiritual people, let us fall on our knees and repent, ever seeking this kind of togetherness, where we can eat and drink together, enacting God's mercy in America. When we have truly done this, we can rejoice, lifting our faces to the rising sun.

SPIRITUAL COMMITMENT

- Reread the Spiritual. How might God be inviting you to deepen your understanding of Holy Eucharist?

- Pay attention to the reading from Deuteronomy and make a list of ten things that would, in your view, make Americans a "wise and discerning people."

- Ask five people in your life what true repentance of the sin of racism would look like.

- In what ways can we seek to transform our worship and our churches so they reflect the full diversity of God's people?

- What does "together" mean for our society today in light of systemic racism? Do you think there is systemic racism in American society?

- What does the phrase "face to the rising sun" mean to you? Where do you find hope in those words?

Ride On, King Jesus

Ride on, King Jesus,
No man can hinder me.
Ride on, King Jesus, ride on,
No man can hinder me.

King Jesus rides a milk-white horse.
No man works like him.
The river Jordan he did cross.
No man works like him.

SCRIPTURE

Joshua 14:6-15

Then the people of Judah came to Joshua at Gilgal; and Caleb son of Jephunneh the Kenizzite said to him, "You know what the LORD said to Moses the man of God in Kadesh-barnea concerning you and me. I was forty years old when Moses the servant of the LORD sent me from Kadesh-barnea to spy out the land; and I brought him an honest report. But my companions who went up with me made the heart of the people melt; yet I wholeheartedly followed the LORD my God. And Moses swore on that day, saying, 'Surely the land on which your foot has trodden shall be an inheritance for you and your children forever, because you have wholeheartedly followed the LORD my God.' And now, as you see, the LORD has kept me alive, as he said, these forty-five years since the time that the LORD spoke this word to Moses, while Israel was journeying through the wilderness; and here I am today, eighty-five years old. I am still as strong today as I was on the day that Moses sent me; my strength now is as my strength was then, for war, and for going and coming. So now give me this hill country of which the LORD spoke on that day; for you heard on that day how the Anakim were there, with great fortified cities; it may be that the LORD will be with me, and I shall drive them out, as the LORD said." Then Joshua blessed him, and gave Hebron to Caleb son of Jephunneh for an inheritance. So Hebron became the inheritance of Caleb son of Jephunneh the Kenizzite to this day, because he wholeheartedly followed the LORD, the God of Israel. Now the name of Hebron formerly was Kiriath-arba; this Arba was the greatest man among the Anakim. And the land had rest from war.

Psalm 34:1-3

I will bless the LORD at all times; his praise shall ever be in my mouth. I will glory in the LORD; let the humble hear and rejoice. Proclaim with me the greatness of the LORD; let us exalt his Name together.

Matthew 6:1-8

"Beware of practicing your piety before others in order to be seen by them; for then you have no reward from your Father in heaven. "So whenever you give alms, do not sound a trumpet before you, as the hypocrites do in the synagogues and in the streets, so that they may be praised by others. Truly I tell you, they have received their reward. But when you give alms, do not let your left hand know what your right hand is doing, so that your alms may be done in secret; and your Father who sees in secret will reward you.

"And whenever you pray, do not be like the hypocrites; for they love to stand and pray in the synagogues and at the street corners, so that they may be seen by others. Truly I tell you, they have received their reward. But whenever you pray, go into your room and shut the door and pray to your Father who is in secret; and your Father who sees in secret will reward you. "When you are praying, do not heap up empty phrases as the Gentiles do; for they think that they will be heard because of their many words. Do not be like them, for your Father knows what you need before you ask him.

SPIRITUAL REFLECTION

Rosa Parks's famous bus ride and the bus boycotts of the Civil Rights movement are at the very heart of this Spiritual. "Ride on" means we all have to keep on keeping on. It's all about perseverance in the present moment. The movement for equality invites us to remember that eternal life is now; we must live and ride on. We must march in support of justice for one another. We are living, spiritual people; you better believe that we have work to do in the area of racism in America and the world.

Ride on, King Jesus. This Spiritual speaks to the confidence the Slaves had in Jesus and certainly echoes the sentiments of spiritual people today. Nothing can hinder the trajectory of Jesus's life or the ultimate victory of good over evil. The mention of the River Jordan invites us to think about our baptism because, in the waters of baptism, we vow to respect the dignity of every human being.

African Americans know that the struggle for justice and peace demands full presence, now, and eyes on the prize. The challenge of achieving racial justice requires focus, commitment, and work in this moment. As long as there is life, all of us have to remain alert to the sin of racism; we have to "ride on" and keep working to eradicate racism and all its effects.

But the hope we have in Jesus reminds us that the victory has already been won. Spiritual people know that the work of salvation calls us to commit to live as the people of God all the way to the end, nonetheless.

The Hebrew Scriptures describe the experience of the people of Israel, showing that their lived experience is a constant struggle to remain faithful to the ways of God. Jesus preached a gospel of love and salvation and called his followers to a steadfast living of love and justice amid struggle, too.

Poverty, incarceration, violence, police brutality, poor health care, and shoddy educational systems throughout the African American communities in the United States today give the sense that little has changed. We look to King Jesus, who rides on unhindered, desires our flourishing, and calls us to be like him.

SPIRITUAL COMMITMENT

- Reread the Spiritual. How might God be calling you to recommit to achieving social justice?

- How do the scriptures invite you to rethink or deepen your response to how we live together as God's family?

- Write a letter to your senator, priest, bishop, or a friend and share your views about what can be done to make race relations better.

- Read a current book on racism in America or join a book group.

- What do you need to persevere in your commitment to racial justice?

Hold On

Hold on just a little while longer.
Hold on just a little while longer.
Everything will be all right.
Keep your hand on that plow—hold on.
Keep your hand on that plow.
Hold on, hold on, hold on.

Pray on just a little while longer.
Pray on just a little while longer.
Everything will be all right.
Keep your hand on that plow—hold on.
Keep your hand on that plow.
Hold on, hold on, hold on.

SCRIPTURE
Ruth 1:15-18

So she said, "See, your sister-in-law has gone back to her people and to her gods; return after your sister-in-law." But Ruth said, "Do not press me to leave you or to turn back from following you! Where you go, I will go; Where you lodge, I will lodge; your people shall be my people, and your God my God. Where you die, I will die—there will I be buried. May the LORD do thus and so to me, and more as well, if even death parts me from you!" When Naomi saw that she was determined to go with her, she said no more to her.

Psalm 37:5-7

Commit your way to the LORD and put your trust in him, and he will bring it to pass. He will make your righteousness as clear as the light and your just dealing as the noonday. Be still before the LORD and wait patiently for him.

Matthew 17:1-9

Six days later, Jesus took with him Peter and James and his brother John and led them up a high mountain, by themselves. And he was transfigured before them, and his face shone like the sun, and his clothes became dazzling white. Suddenly there appeared to them Moses and Elijah, talking with him. Then Peter said to Jesus, "Lord, it is good for us to be here; if you wish, I will make three dwellings here, one for you, one for Moses, and one for Elijah." While he was still speaking, suddenly a bright cloud overshadowed them, and from the cloud a voice said, "This is my Son, the Beloved; with him I am well pleased; listen to him!" When the disciples heard this, they fell to the ground and were overcome by fear. But Jesus came and touched them, saying, "Get up and do not be afraid." And when they looked up, they saw no one except Jesus himself alone. As they were coming down the mountain, Jesus ordered them, "Tell no one about the vision until after the Son of Man has been raised from the dead."

SPIRITUAL REFLECTION

When the African people were captured, bought, sold, and carried to America, they deepened their ability to communicate in code. They had to protect their lives by signaling in discreet and undetectable ways. "Hold on" and "pray on" are code words embedded in the Spiritual. For instance, "pray on" could be a signal to meet in order to plan an escape. The Black Lives Matter movement challenges all of us to hold on to what is just, respectful, and truthful as if our lives depend upon it. The Black Lives Matter movement insists that we pray on, as Jesus did, unto his death. "Just a little while longer" is all we need, and we must keep our hands on the plow.

Hold on just a little while longer. Pray on just a little while longer. Dr. Martin Luther King Jr. always reminded those who listened to him to hold on and pray on. He also preached that people who believe in something have to be willing to march for it and work for it, too.

The virtues of faith and hope in the Christian life possessed by the Slaves gave them strength to believe that one day, "everything will be all right." Believing that everything will be all right is a powerful and prophetic spiritual virtue. The marches throughout many of our cities during the spring of 2020 show a desire of the Black Lives Matter movement to remind the American people to hold on and to pray on, to march on with clarity that justice will come.

Many Americans indicate that they are aware that African Americans are treated more harshly by the police than White Americans. African Americans and other people of color talk about the fear they have when their children go out to play or to school or to work. It is a sad reality that the American dream is denied to some Americans. African Americans feel that America has not been America to them.

Amidst all the suffering, pain, and death, African Americans still call us to join in singing this Spiritual, believing that, if we work together as one, we can extend the true American dream to all of America.

The story of Ruth reminds us that God calls us to commit to each other even in our differences. It is a call to remember that we are one family, one in the Spirit. And in the psalm assigned for today, we hear the invitation to commit to the way of the Lord. Commitment to God requires that we keep our hands on the plow, hold on and pray on as one. We can do this together.

SPIRITUAL COMMITMENT

- Reread the Spiritual. How might God be calling you to hold on and pray on?

- How do the scriptures invite you to think about your ongoing commitment to the issues facing the African American community?

- Visit an African American church online or in person or listen to one of the speeches of Dr. King.

- Read the Spiritual or one of the scriptures with your family or a friend and discuss what it can teach about the Black Lives Matter movement.

- What will you do to put your faith into action today?

Do Lord, Remember Me

Do Lord, do Lord, do Lord,
Remember me.
Do Lord, do Lord, do Lord,
Remember me.
Do Lord, do Lord, do Lord,
Remember me.
Look away beyond the blue.

When I am in trouble,
Do Lord, do Lord, do Lord,
Remember me.
Do Lord, do Lord, do Lord,
Remember me.
Look away beyond the blue.

SCRIPTURE

Isaiah 6:1-8

In the year that King Uzziah died, I saw the Lord sitting on a throne, high and lofty; and the hem of his robe filled the temple. Seraphs were in attendance above him; each had six wings: with two they covered their faces, and with two they covered their feet, and with two they flew. And one called to another and said: "Holy, holy, holy is the LORD of hosts; the whole earth is full of his glory." The pivots on the thresholds shook at the voices of those who called, and the house filled with smoke.

And I said: "Woe is me! I am lost, for I am a man of unclean lips, and I live among a people of unclean lips; yet my eyes have seen the King, the LORD of hosts!" Then one of the seraphs flew to me, holding a live coal that had been taken from the altar with a pair of tongs. The seraph touched my mouth with it and said: "Now that this has touched your lips, your guilt has departed and your sin is blotted out." Then I heard the voice of the Lord saying, "Whom shall I send, and who will go for us?" And I said, "Here am I; send me!"

Psalm 43:1-2

Give judgment for me, O God, and defend my cause against an ungodly people; deliver me from the deceitful and the wicked. For you are the God of my strength; why have you put me from you? And why do I go so heavily while the enemy oppresses me?

Matthew 23:27-39

"Woe to you, scribes and Pharisees, hypocrites! For you are like whitewashed tombs, which on the outside look beautiful, but inside they are full of the bones of the dead and of all kinds of filth. So you also on the outside look righteous to others, but inside you are full of hypocrisy and lawlessness. "Woe to you, scribes and Pharisees, hypocrites! For you build the tombs of the prophets and decorate the graves of the righteous, and you say, 'If we had lived in the days of our ancestors, we would not have taken part with them in shedding the blood of the prophets.' Thus you testify against yourselves that you are descendants of those who murdered the prophets. Fill up, then, the measure of your ancestors. You snakes, you brood of vipers! How can you escape being sentenced to hell?

Therefore I send you prophets, sages, and scribes, some of whom you will kill and crucify, and some you will flog in your synagogues and pursue from town to town, so that upon you may come all the righteous blood shed on earth, from the blood of righteous Abel to the blood of Zechariah son of Barachiah, whom you murdered between the sanctuary and the altar. Truly I tell you, all this will come upon this generation. "Jerusalem, Jerusalem, the city that kills the prophets and stones those who are sent to it! How often have I desired to gather your children together as a hen gathers her brood under her wings, and you were not willing! See, your house is left to you, desolate. For I tell you, you will not see me again until you say, 'Blessed is the one who comes in the name of the Lord.'"

SPIRITUAL REFLECTION

The movement for justice and equality for African Americans calls America to remember its own Constitution, the scriptures, and our common heritage of humanity as God's own. When we remember who we are and whose we are in God, we will love and respect each other more deeply. Our prayers and supplication to God, in which we ask God to remember us in God's mercy, are invoked in this Spiritual.

Do Lord, do Lord, remember. In truth, there is no more powerful prayer than this one. The Slaves wanted God to remember them the way God remembered the enslaved Israelites and the Crucified Christ. The Slaves echoed the cry of the thief who is crucified next to Jesus, the one who asks Jesus to remember him when Jesus comes into his reign.

When in our suffering we ask God to remember us, we are committing to remember the suffering of others also. The cry from the Spiritual is an indictment of the slave masters who don't seem to remember who God is and what God asks of humanity.

This Spiritual is also more than just a song; it is a creed. In this creed, the Slaves affirm a faith in the God who remembers them. Though God is "beyond the blue," they also know that God in Christ is with them and in them.

Every Sunday and at every eucharist, we hear the words of Jesus: *Do this in memory of me.* Jesus wants us to remember him, Jesus pleads with us to remember him.

How do we remember Jesus? We remember Jesus by working for justice and peace. We remember Jesus by taking on the mind and memory of Christ, which call us to serve one another, wash each other's feet, and remember that we are all God's children.

When I am in trouble, do Lord, remember me. There is a lot of trouble in the world, and America is in trouble because of the sin of racism. Remember: our call as a eucharistic people is clear.

SPIRITUAL COMMITMENT

- Reread the Spiritual. How might God be calling you to remember who you are and whose you are?

- How do the scriptures invite you to remember the troubles of racism facing the African American community?

- Spend some time today and make a list of ten ways in which racism manifests in your life, the church, or society.

- Read the Spiritual or one of the scriptures with your family or a friend and discuss a Christian response to racial justice in America.

- What will you do today to remember the suffering of others?

Knees On Our Lives

You have your knees on our lives.
Knees on our heads—all this time
Knees on our necks—all this time
Knees on our chests—all this time
Knees on our bellies—all this time
Knees on our groins—all this time
Knees on our private parts
Knees on our backsides
Knees on our thighs
Knees on our legs and feet
Knees on our hands.
All this time.

Our Black bodies can't breathe.
We will not take it anymore
We want to live
We want to breathe
Our minds and our souls like
Phoenix rising
Sankofa and be free
Rising and flying away this bright morning
Rising. Flying.
Those knees
like chains
We will break
for wings.

O Mary, Don't You Weep

O Mary, don't you weep, don't you mourn.
O Mary, don't you weep, don't you mourn.
Pharaoh's children are fallen.
O Mary, don't you weep, don't you mourn.

O Mary, don't you weep, don't you mourn.
O Mary, don't you weep, don't you mourn.
Pharaoh's children are drowned.
O Mary, don't you weep, don't you mourn.

SCRIPTURE

Isaiah 9:2-7

The people who walked in darkness have seen a great light; those who lived in a land of deep darkness—on them light has shined. You have multiplied the nation, you have increased its joy; they rejoice before you as with joy at the harvest, as people exult when dividing plunder. For the yoke of their burden, and the bar across their shoulders, the rod of their oppressor, you have broken as on the day of Midian. For all the boots of the tramping warriors and all the garments rolled in blood shall be burned as fuel for the fire. For a child has been born for us, a son given to us; authority rests upon his shoulders; and he is named Wonderful Counselor, Mighty God, Everlasting Father, Prince of Peace. His authority shall grow continually, and there shall be endless peace for the throne of David and his kingdom. He will establish and uphold it with justice and with righteousness from this time onward and forevermore. The zeal of the LORD of hosts will do this.

Psalm 44:17-18, 20-22

All this has come upon us; yet we have not forgotten you, nor have we betrayed your covenant. Our heart never turned back, nor did our footsteps stray from your path.... If we have forgotten the Name of our God, or stretched out our hands to some strange god, will not God find it out? For he knows the secrets of the heart. Indeed, for your sake we are killed all the day long; we are accounted as sheep for the slaughter.

Matthew 25:31-46

"When the Son of Man comes in his glory, and all the angels with him, then he will sit on the throne of his glory. All the nations will be gathered before him, and he will separate people one from another as a shepherd separates the sheep from the goats, and he will put the sheep at his right hand and the goats at the left. Then the king will say to those at his right hand, 'Come, you that are blessed by my Father, inherit the kingdom prepared for you from the foundation of the world; for I was hungry and you gave me food, I was thirsty and you gave me something to drink, I was a stranger and you welcomed me, I was naked and you gave me clothing, I was sick and you took care of me, I was in prison and you visited me.' Then the righteous will answer him, 'Lord, when was it that we saw you hungry and gave you food, or thirsty and gave you something to drink? And when was it that we saw you a stranger and welcomed you, or naked and gave you clothing? And when was it that we saw you sick or in prison and visited you?' And the king will answer them, 'Truly I tell you, just as you did it to one of the least of these who are members of my family, you did it to me.' Then he will say to those at his left hand, 'You that are accursed, depart from me into the eternal fire prepared for the devil and his angels; for I was hungry and you gave me no food, I was thirsty and you gave me nothing to drink, I was a stranger and you did not welcome me, naked and you did not give me clothing, sick and in prison and you did not visit me.' Then they also will answer, 'Lord, when was it that we saw you hungry or thirsty or a stranger or naked or sick or in prison, and did not take care of you?' Then he will answer them, 'Truly I tell you, just as you did not do it to one of the least of these, you did not do it to me.' And these will go away into eternal punishment, but the righteous into eternal life."

SPIRITUAL REFLECTION

Liberation theology, a way of thinking about God popularized in Latin America in the 1950's and 1960's, emphasizes liberation of oppressed peoples and a preferential option for the poor, calling the church to pay special attention to those in poverty. From this foundation, liberation theologians contend that the crisis facing the Christian faith is that Christians and people of faith are dying before their time. They go further to state that, oftentimes, the people are dying before their time at the hands of Christians.

"O Mary, Don't You Weep" speaks to the reality of weeping mothers in America. The Spiritual also speaks in comforting words to the reality of what the Slaves experienced. In their suffering, they comforted each other. In their pain, they found ways to console each other and to remind one another that their weeping was not in vain.

Pharaoh's children are fallen. Pharaoh's children are drowned. The faith of the Slaves assured them that God would liberate them and punish their enemies. Their faith gave them hope that, although they might not see the power of God's liberation in their lifetime, God would rescue them.

The Slaves were not simply saying, "Don't cry." They were acknowledging the pain and suffering, but they could see that Easter came after Good Friday.

Of course, at times, it is no real comfort to say to those who mourn that they should not cry. We who have experienced death know that grief has a life of its own. However, we also know that God comes to us in our suffering, comforts us, and gives us hope.

For African Americans, there is a strong belief that the racism of Pharaoh can be toppled. The marches, letters, writings, and demonstrations associated with the fight for justice from the time of the Slaves to the present moment speak to an unwavering belief that the God who liberates marches with those who seek justice. God is a God of life and justice. The systemic racism and the ongoing effects of discrimination and injustice do not play a part in God's plan for the world. We who believe that in Jesus Christ, God has redeemed the world must continue to stand up for God's reign of peace, justice, and love. In our commitment to address the suffering and death that are evident in our country, we declare to the world, in one way or another, that Pharaoh has fallen and drowned.

SPIRITUAL COMMITMENT

- Reread the Spiritual. How might God be calling you to weep with those who weep?

- How do the scriptures invite you to think about the suffering in this world, especially the suffering caused by racism?

- Think of people or situations in your life where you could be a source of comfort. Make a list and commit to carrying out an act of comfort or more.

- Read the Spiritual or one of the scripture passages and, perhaps, find a video of one of the mothers whose sons were killed by the police. Bear witness to her agony and notice what comes up in you as a result of your solidarity.

- Who is Mary in your life? Where and why is she weeping?

Come by Here, My Lord

Come by here, my Lord,
Come by here.
Come by here, my Lord,
Come by here.

Someone's crying, Lord,
Come by here.
Someone's crying, Lord.
Come by here.
Someone's crying, Lord.
Come by here.

Someone's dying, Lord.
Come by here, my Lord.
Come by here.
Come by here, my Lord.
Come by here.

Someone's living, Lord.
Come by here, my Lord.
Come by here.
Come by here, my Lord.
Come by here.

SCRIPTURE

Jeremiah 1:4-10

Now the word of the LORD came to me saying, "Before I formed you in the womb I knew you, and before you were born I consecrated you; I appointed you a prophet to the nations." Then I said, "Ah, Lord GOD! Truly I do not know how to speak, for I am only a boy." But the LORD said to me,

"Do not say, 'I am only a boy'; for you shall go to all to whom I send you, and you shall speak whatever I command you, Do not be afraid of them, for I am with you to deliver you, says the LORD." Then the LORD put out his hand and touched my mouth; and the LORD said to me, "Now I have put my words in your mouth. See, today I appoint you over nations and over kingdoms, to pluck up and to pull down, to destroy and to overthrow, to build and to plant."

Psalm 46:1-3

God is our refuge and strength, a very present help in trouble. Therefore we will not fear, though the earth be moved, and though the mountains be toppled into the depths of the sea; though its waters rage and foam, and though the mountains tremble at its tumult.

Mark 2:1-12

When he returned to Capernaum after some days, it was reported that he was at home. So many gathered around that there was no longer room for them, not even in front of the door; and he was speaking the word to them. Then some people came, bringing to him a paralyzed man, carried by four of them. And when they could not bring him to Jesus because of the crowd, they removed the roof above him; and after having dug through it, they let down the mat on which the paralytic lay. When Jesus saw their faith, he said to the paralytic, "Son, your sins are forgiven." Now some of the scribes were sitting there, questioning in their hearts, "Why does this fellow speak in this way? It is blasphemy! Who can forgive sins but God alone?" At once Jesus perceived in his spirit that they were discussing these questions among themselves; and he said to them, "Why do you raise such questions in your hearts? Which is easier, to say to the paralytic, 'Your sins are forgiven,' or to say, 'Stand up and take your mat and walk'? But so that you may know that the Son of Man has authority on earth to forgive sins"—he said to the paralytic—"I say to you, stand up, take your mat and go to your home." And he stood up, and immediately took the mat and went out before all of them; so that they were all amazed and glorified God, saying, "We have never seen anything like this!"

SPIRITUAL REFLECTION

It is said that every protest movement is a call for justice and peace to become incarnate. In one African story, it is said that every time one protests, God comes down to watch, God draws near. I have joined many of the Black Lives Matter marches throughout New York City. I have never heard them sing this Spiritual, but I can attest that this request for God's presence is what the marches are all about. *God, in your justice and mercy and love, come by here.*

"Come by Here, My Lord" shows a sophisticated Christian theology. When we sing this Spiritual, we should not miss the insistence that God comes to meet us, that God is Lord, and that our lived experience of God is that God responds. This is indeed the Christian life, expressed right here in this Spiritual.

In addition, the call to God to come by is a reminder that we as spiritual people, we who follow Jesus, must be present to the suffering and realities of our brothers and sisters. We do well to remember that we are the image and likeness of God. We are God's presence in the world, and we need to come by the suffering and pain of others. What we do to the least, we do to God.

Many of us learned a similar children's chorus, "Come into my heart, Lord Jesus. Come in today, come in to stay." Similarly, the Spiritual of the day, at times called Kumbaya, reveals an expectant confidence that God will come by and address the issues of the day. There is nothing more radical than inviting God to come by and be near us.

The faith of the Slaves was strong enough for them to invite God into their horrible situation. When they were crying, dying, and trying to survive day to day, still they sought God. In this sense, the Slaves demonstrated a powerful grasp of incarnational theology: God is the God who comes by "here."

My mother often got upset if I invited friends to the house without advance warning, because, to her mind, she didn't have time to prepare the house properly. The subversive nature of this Spiritual is this: if the United States creates conditions of inhumanity, diminishment, squalor, suffering, and death, then that is the reality into which Jesus will be invited to stay. Jesus meets us where we are.

SPIRITUAL COMMITMENT

- Reread the Spiritual. What is the "here" in America today?

- How do the scriptures call you to invite God into the reality of your life and the challenges in American society?

- Spend some time in meditation today on the fact that, because of the effects of the sin of racism, people are crying, dying, and trying to survive, here, day by day. Think about the realities facing African American communities.

- What do the scriptures have to teach us about our ongoing obligation to each other, especially African Americans?

- How might you be the presence of God in a racially charged world?

Sometimes I Feel
Like a Motherless Child

Sometimes I feel like a motherless child.
Sometimes I feel like a motherless child.
Sometimes I feel like a motherless child.
A long way from home,
A long way from home.
Then I get down on my knees and pray.
Get down on my knees and pray.

Sometimes I feel like I'm almost gone.
Sometimes I feel like I'm almost gone.
Sometimes I feel like I'm almost gone.
A long way from home,
A long way from home.
Then I get down on my knees and pray.
Get down on my knees and pray.

SCRIPTURE
Daniel 2:36-45

"This was the dream; now we will tell the king its interpretation. You, O king, the king of kings—to whom the God of heaven has given the kingdom, the power, the might, and the glory, into whose hand he has given human beings, wherever they live, the wild animals of the field, and the birds of the air, and whom he has established as ruler over them all—you are the head of gold. After you shall arise another kingdom inferior to yours, and yet a third kingdom of bronze, which shall rule over the whole earth. And there shall be a fourth kingdom, strong as iron; just as iron crushes and smashes everything, it shall crush and shatter all these.

As you saw the feet and toes partly of potter's clay and partly of iron, it shall be a divided kingdom; but some of the strength of iron shall be in it, as you saw the iron mixed with the clay. As the toes of the feet were part iron and part clay, so the kingdom shall be partly strong and partly brittle. As you saw the iron mixed with clay, so will they mix with one another in marriage, but they will not hold together, just as iron does not mix with clay. And in the days of those kings the God of heaven will set up a kingdom that shall never be destroyed, nor shall this kingdom be left to another people. It shall crush all these kingdoms and bring them to an end, and it shall stand forever; just as you saw that a stone was cut from the mountain not by hands, and that it crushed the iron, the bronze, the clay, the silver, and the gold. The great God has informed the king what shall be hereafter. The dream is certain, and its interpretation trustworthy."

Psalm 51:7-10

For behold, you look for truth deep within me, and will make me understand wisdom secretly. Purge me from my sin, and I shall be pure; wash me, and I shall be clean indeed. Make me hear of joy and gladness, that the body you have broken may rejoice. Hide your face from my sins and blot out all my iniquities.

Mark 3:19b-35

Then he went home; and the crowd came together again, so that they could not even eat. When his family heard it, they went out to restrain him, for people were saying, "He has gone out of his mind." And the scribes who came down from Jerusalem said, "He has Beelzebul, and by the ruler of the demons he casts out demons." And he called them to him, and spoke to them in parables, "How can Satan cast out Satan? If a kingdom is divided against itself, that kingdom cannot stand. And if a house is divided against itself, that house will not be able to stand. And if Satan has risen up against himself and is divided, he cannot stand, but his end has come. But no one can enter a strong man's house and plunder his property without first tying up the strong man; then indeed the house can be plundered."

"Truly I tell you, people will be forgiven for their sins and whatever blasphemies they utter; but whoever blasphemes against the Holy Spirit can never have forgiveness, but is guilty of an eternal sin"—for they had said, "He has an unclean spirit."

Then his mother and his brothers came; and standing outside, they sent to him and called him. A crowd was sitting around him; and they said to him, "Your mother and your brothers and sisters are outside, asking for you." And he replied, "Who are my mother and my brothers?" And looking at those who sat around him, he said, "Here are my mother and my brothers! Whoever does the will of God is my brother and sister and mother."

SPIRITUAL REFLECTION

An early proclamation in the African American struggle for equal rights and justice was the cry, "I am a Man." Imagine any human being, from any human group, having to make a declaration. Yet, the sin of racism continues to provoke what should be obvious to all: that humans are humans and should be treated as such. This means all humans, not just some.

As Christians and spiritual people, we accept that every person is made in the image and likeness of God. We are all children of God, made in love, made by love, and made to love each other. One of our primary tasks as people of God is to acknowledge that every human being deserves respect and love. Throughout the teachings of Jesus is the call to love God and love our neighbor. Jesus taught that unless we recognize each other as children of God, we cannot recognize or know God. The task, therefore, is for Christians to work toward a world where we exist as family, a world in which we are all each other's brother, sister, father, friend, and mother.

Sometimes, I feel like a motherless child. These words stir up powerful emotions within our hearts. Many of us have been blessed with a loving mother, and that love has made all the difference in our adult lives. Some of us know the unhealed wound of an unavailable mother or the pain that comes from losing our mother.

In slavery, the reality of being a motherless child was quite common. Slaves were the property of their masters, and their masters had absolute power over the family of the Slaves. During the time of slavery, it was common practice to take the child away from the mother and send the child to another plantation. Separating children from their families is an ugly and ancient practice used to control people and send a message of domination by breaking deep connections.

Somehow, in their resilience, the Slaves learned to manage and live with many realities, even conflicting ones. Many of the Slaves were motherless (ripped from their mothers at a young age), and many had had to leave their mothers behind in Africa. Many were motherless and fatherless, but there was also a reality that must not be forgotten: the Slaves found ways of maintaining the sense of tribe and community. Though many were motherless, few lived without a sense of communal family.

One of the things that was foundational for the Slaves who believed in God was an unshakeable faith in the power of prayer during the most difficult times and under the most inhuman conditions. When any felt like a motherless child or that their life was slipping away, their faith in God sustained them.

SPIRITUAL COMMITMENT

- Reread the Spiritual. How do your personal losses and suffering make you more compassionate?

- How do the scriptures challenge you to respond to a culture that makes people motherless? Who is your mother?

- Think about your family values and examine how these values call you to view the American society, especially African Americans in American Society.

- Think about how we perpetuate the experience of "motherless child" in our society today through policies and practices that fail children.

- What causes you to fall on your knees and pray?

Babylon, You Gone Down

Babylon, you gone down.
Babylon, you gone down.
Babylon, you gone.
Babylon, you gone.
And your throne gone down.

Oppressor man, you gone.
Oppressor man, you gone.
Oppressor man, you gone.
And your throne gone down.

SCRIPTURE

Micah 6:6-8

"With what shall I come before the LORD, and bow myself before God on high? Shall I come before him with burnt offerings, with calves a year old? Will the LORD be pleased with thousands of rams, with ten thousands of rivers of oil? Shall I give my firstborn for my transgression, the fruit of my body for the sin of my soul?" He has told you, O mortal, what is good; and what does the LORD require of you but to do justice, and to love kindness, and to walk humbly with your God?

Psalm 54:4-5

Behold, God is my helper; it is the Lord who sustains my life. Render evil to those who spy on me; in your faithfulness, destroy them.

Mark 4:26-34

He also said, "The kingdom of God is as if someone would scatter seed on the ground, and would sleep and rise night and day, and the seed would sprout and grow, he does not know how. The earth produces of itself, first the stalk, then the head, then the full grain in the head. But when the grain is ripe, at once he goes in with his sickle, because the harvest has come."

He also said, "With what can we compare the kingdom of God, or what parable will we use for it? It is like a mustard seed, which, when sown upon the ground, is the smallest of all the seeds on earth; yet when it is sown it grows up and becomes the greatest of all shrubs, and puts forth large branches, so that the birds of the air can make nests in its shade."

With many such parables he spoke the word to them, as they were able to hear it; he did not speak to them except in parables, but he explained everything in private to his disciples.

SPIRITUAL REFLECTION

This Spiritual is widely known in Jamaica, but less so in the United States of America. In this case, the term Babylon describes societal and structural "sin" and is used synonymously to describe structures of oppression and racism. African Americans have long lamented their experience of feeling that the laws and structures of society are never in their favor. Since the time of slavery up to the present moment, African Americans have devoted themselves to naming and pointing out the injustices in the culture and judicial systems that work against them.

The Black Lives Matter movement is focused on naming the structural and systemic racism in the history of America. The Black Lives Matter movement is committed to overthrowing the systems that perpetuate suffering and killing today.

"Babylon, You Gone Down" celebrates the reality that Babylon has fallen. In truth, we all know deep down that evil will never triumph, in the same way that death never has the last word. Babylon is forever going down, even though it makes its evil and suffering felt along the way.

To understand more fully the world of the Spirituals, one needs to study the horrors of the organized slave trade. When Europeans organized in a unified effort to capture and dominate the peoples from Africa, they developed a culture and a structure that institutionalized the treatment of Africans like animals—the structural racism had as its goal the dehumanization of the African Slaves.

To sing, fight, and protest for justice is to hold at the very same time a profound belief that things will change for the better. Of course, Babylon and all institutions of power do not release their hold on the status quo easily; still, knowing that love will always defeat hate is a great faith to exercise. There is also no denying that the life of Jesus shows him explicitly condemning the oppressive structures of his day. Jesus also taught his followers to act against the systems of oppression as he taught them that he came to bring life and freedom to all.

The second verse in the Spiritual addresses the masters of the Slaves most directly: "Oppressor man, you gone and your throne gone down." Again, the power and wisdom of those who sang the Spirituals is in the recognition that structural oppression is always expressed through individuals. Their vision of a time after oppression was as certain. We are called to remember that sin has faces, and systemic racism has people devoted to maintaining the status quo.

Reminiscent of Jesus saying that he saw Satan fall from heaven, this Spiritual affirms that with each passing day, no matter how bleak the reality may look, racism cannot prevail. The ugliness, the killings, and the death caused by racism have "gone down" and will continue to fall until things are made right. Yes, we are a people who believe that God has redeemed the world. To believe this, we have to live into the call and challenge of dismantling the system of Babylon.

SPIRITUAL COMMITMENT

- Reread the Spiritual. What do you think about the persistent nature of the structural sin of racism?

- How do the scriptures invite you to participate in the fall of systemic racism?

- Devote some time this week to reading about the inhumane realities of slavery.

- Read the Spiritual or one of the scriptures and think about how the "kingdom of God" is different from Babylon (i.e., what justice looks like.)

- What steps can you take to become a stronger ally in the fight to defeat structural racism in the church and society?

We Shall Overcome

We shall overcome.
We shall overcome.
We shall overcome someday.
Deep in my heart,
I do believe
We shall overcome someday.

We shall overcome.
We shall overcome.
We shall overcome today.
Deep in my heart,
I do believe
We shall overcome today.

SCRIPTURE
Malachi 1:6-14

A son honors his father, and servants their master. If then I am a father, where is the honor due me? And if I am a master, where is the respect due me? says the Lord of hosts to you, O priests, who despise my name. You say, "How have we despised your name?" By offering polluted food on my altar. And you say, "How have we polluted it?" By thinking that the Lord's table may be despised. When you offer blind animals in sacrifice, is that not wrong? And when you offer those that are lame or sick, is that not wrong? Try presenting that to your governor; will he be pleased with you or show you favor? says the Lord of hosts. And now implore the favor of God, that he may be gracious to us. The fault is yours. Will he show favor to any of you? says the Lord of hosts. Oh, that someone among you would shut the temple doors, so that you would not kindle fire on my altar in vain! I have no pleasure in you, says the Lord of hosts, and I will not accept an offering from your hands. For from the rising of the sun to its setting my name is great among the nations, and in every place incense is offered to my name, and a pure offering; for my name is great among the nations, says the Lord of hosts. But you profane it when you say that the Lord's table is polluted, and the food for it may be despised. "What a weariness this is," you say, and you sniff at me, says the Lord of hosts. You bring what has been taken by violence or is lame or sick, and this you bring as your offering! Shall I accept that from your hand? says the Lord. Cursed be the cheat who has a male in the flock and vows to give it, and yet sacrifices to the Lord what is blemished; for I am a great King, says the Lord of hosts, and my name is reverenced among the nations.

Psalm 56:10

In God the LORD, whose word I praise, in God I trust and will not be afraid, for what can mortals do to me?

Mark 6:14-29

King Herod heard of it, for Jesus's name had become known. Some were saying, "John the baptizer has been raised from the dead; and for this reason these powers are at work in him." But others said, "It is Elijah." And others said, "It is a prophet, like one of the prophets of old." But when Herod heard of it, he said, "John, whom I beheaded, has been raised."

For Herod himself had sent men who arrested John, bound him, and put him in prison on account of Herodias, his brother Philip's wife, because Herod had married her. For John had been telling Herod, "It is not lawful for you to have your brother's wife." And Herodias had a grudge against him, and wanted to kill him. But she could not, for Herod feared John, knowing that he was a righteous and holy man, and he protected him. When he heard him, he was greatly perplexed; and yet he liked to listen to him. But an opportunity came when Herod on his birthday gave a banquet for his courtiers and officers and for the leaders of Galilee. When his daughter Herodias came in and danced, she pleased Herod and his guests; and the king said to the girl, "Ask me for whatever you wish, and I will give it." And he solemnly swore to her, "Whatever you ask me, I will give you, even half of my kingdom." She went out and said to her mother, "What should I ask for?" She replied, "The head of John the baptizer." Immediately she rushed back to the king and requested, "I want you to give me at once the head of John the Baptist on a platter." The king was deeply grieved; yet out of regard for his oaths and for the guests, he did not want to refuse her. Immediately the king sent a soldier of the guard with orders to bring John's head. He went and beheaded him in the prison, brought his head on a platter, and gave it to the girl. Then the girl gave it to her mother. When his disciples heard about it, they came and took his body, and laid it in a tomb.

SPIRITUAL REFLECTION

Every movement has its founders and seers. The Slave experience and the clarity of purpose of Dr. Martin Luther King Jr. are the foundation for and the prophets of the Black Lives Matter movement. When we think about the fight for racial justice and peace, we must never forget that from the moment of the first African captured, the desire to proclaim Black Lives Matter came to life.

One of the most powerful speeches made by Dr. King was one in which he used "We Shall Overcome" as a repeating refrain. "We Shall Overcome," he said, is a song he and other prisoners chose to sing. He believed that even when we are dismissed as troublemakers and rabblerousers, we should commit our very lives to the belief that we shall overcome.

At one point in his speech, he said, "We shall overcome because the Bible is right!" He went on to say that sometimes we have tears in our eyes, but we must keep on singing. Before this movement is done, he said, we may face being imprisoned, but we shall overcome. Even in the face of death, Dr. King reminded us that death does not have the last word and that we who work for justice must never forget that we will overcome.

As Dr. King preached, "the arc of the moral universe is long, but it bends toward justice." We shall overcome. God will never abandon us in our personal struggles against sin or whatever difficulties we may face. We can count on God to join us in our struggle toward justice. This is our faith. This is what we believe: in God and with God, we shall overcome.

We shall overcome, deep in my heart, I do believe. When something is deep in one's heart, the courage and love in that person's heart protects it from attack. This indomitable belief is what fuels the march for justice. The Slaves knew that there was no way that God supported the lie of their enslavement, and they knew that the lie of oppression would die.

Dr. King believed in his heart that no matter the human loss, physical death, or emotional suffering, African Americans would overcome every last attempt of the oppressor to justify their racist treatment. Truth crushed to earth will rise again, and so, in the words of the Slaves and Dr. King, we shall overcome, and one day, this will be a greater America for it. This Spiritual is a gift to all believers, reminding us that in God we have the victory. Our baptism, our worship, our scriptures, and our lives as Christians call us into this fellowship of acting on the truth that proclaims that we shall overcome.

SPIRITUAL COMMITMENT

- Reread the Spiritual. What are your thoughts about how we are overcoming racism? What preparation does your heart need to sustain your trust?

- How do the scriptures invite you to believe that we shall overcome?

- Spend some time listening to the speech from Dr. King in which he uses the refrain, "We shall overcome." Think about the realities facing African American communities today and all that needs to be overcome.

- Read the Spiritual or one of the scriptures with your family or a friend and discuss what helps you to maintain your firm belief that good will overcome evil.

- How might you participate more deeply in committed acts of justice?

Steal Away

Steal away,
Steal away,
Steal away to Jesus.
Steal away,
Steal away home.
I ain't got long to stay here.

My Lord calls me.
He calls me by the thunder.
The trumpet sounds within my soul.
I ain't got long to stay here.

SCRIPTURE

Romans 3:9-18

What then? Are we any better off? No, not at all; for we have already charged that all, both Jews and Greeks, are under the power of sin, as it is written: "There is no one who is righteous, not even one; there is one who has understanding, there is no one who seeks God. All have turned aside, together they have become worthless; there is no one who shows kindness, there is not even one." "Their throats are opened graves; they use their tongues to deceive." "The venom of vipers is under their lips." "Their mouths are full of cursing and bitterness." "Their feet are swift to shed blood; ruin and misery are in their paths, and the way of peace they have not known." "There is no fear of God before their eyes."

Psalm 59:3-5

See how they lie in wait for my life, how the mighty gather together against me; not for any offense or fault of mine, O Lord. Not because of any guilt of mine they run and prepare themselves for battle. Rouse yourself, come to my side, and see; for you, Lord God of hosts, are Israel's God.

Mark 7:24-30

From there he set out and went away to the region of Tyre. He entered a house and did not want anyone to know he was there. Yet he could not escape notice, but a woman whose little daughter had an unclean spirit immediately heard about him, and she came and bowed down at his feet. Now the woman was a Gentile, of Syrophoenician origin. She begged him to cast the demon out of her daughter. He said to her, "Let the children be fed first, for it is not fair to take the children's food and throw it to the dogs." But she answered him, "Sir, even the dogs under the table eat the children's crumbs." Then he said to her, "For saying that, you may go—the demon has left your daughter." So she went home, found the child lying on the bed, and the demon gone.

SPIRITUAL REFLECTION

An important message of the Christian life is that we are called to be free in all aspects of our lives. Sin enslaves us psychologically, emotionally, spiritually, and even physically. When we pay attention to the teachings of Jesus, we see a clear call for us to resist temptation, resist the devil, and to "steal away" from the things that entrap us. Jesus embodied this teaching by the miracles and healings that he did. In every encounter with those who felt trapped by disease, cultural traditions, or sin, Jesus set those he encountered free.

One message of the Black Lives Matter movement proclaims the need for all of America to move away from actions that cause harm, suffering, and death to African Americans. It is a message that calls all people of goodwill to steal away from the systems of oppression and racism and get to a place where there is justice and peace. On many levels, this message echoes the call of all spiritual movements in its insistence that as human beings, we can always do and be better.

The words, "Steal away, steal away to Jesus. I ain't got long to stay here," speak to the growing realization of the Slaves that slavery was not where they belonged. Of course, some Slaves remembered their lives before enslavement in Africa, and they knew they were not created to live and exist in cruel and subhuman conditions. Living in bondage and longing to be free required a lot of courage, and there were Slaves who preferred death to bondage. In this sense, we can see many possible meanings to "steal away" in the Spiritual.

In the words of this Spiritual, the Slaves linked their desire for freedom to Jesus himself. For them, Jesus was the Savior who would welcome them in stealing away. For them, it was Jesus calling them to steal away, and they knew that in Jesus they had a safe refuge.

"My Lord calls me" affirms a radical and a prophetic belief in Jesus and is a message that all of us need to hear today. Jesus calls us into freedom and abundant life. For the Slaves, the message of Jesus for them was crystal clear: God did not create them to be enslaved, and they needed to steal away.

With such a long and strong legacy of racism in American life, there is no wonder that racism is deeply ingrained. Many Black and Brown Americans bear the burden of both explicit and implicit racism at their jobs, in churches, and elsewhere. In truth, every day, there is a yearning for many African Americans to steal away. "The trumpet sounds within my soul" shows the urgent realization and the undeniability of the call to be free from oppression.

SPIRITUAL COMMITMENT

- Reread the Spiritual. How are you being called to "steal away" in these times?

- How do the scriptures invite you into listening more deeply to God about God's dream for abundant life for all?

- Spend some time reflecting on a moment in your life when you had to "steal away to Jesus" and the cost of doing that. If you have never done that, do it.

- Do some journaling or make some art today using the Spiritual and the scriptures as a way of dialoguing with the concerns of the Black Lives Matter movement.

- What do the words, "I ain't got long to stay here," evoke in you?

This Little Light of Mine

This little light of mine,
I'm gonna let it shine.
This little light of mine.
I'm gonna let it shine.
This little light of mine,
I'm gonna let it shine.

Let it shine, let it shine, let it shine.

SCRIPTURE
Romans 8:18-27

I consider that the sufferings of this present time are not worth comparing with the glory about to be revealed to us. For the creation waits with eager longing for the revealing of the children of God; for the creation was subjected to futility, not of its own will but by the will of the one who subjected it, in hope that the creation itself will be set free from its bondage to decay and will obtain the freedom of the glory of the children of God. We know that the whole creation has been groaning in labor pains until now; and not only the creation, but we ourselves, who have the first fruits of the Spirit, groan inwardly while we wait for adoption, the redemption of our bodies. For in hope we were saved. Now hope that is seen is not hope. For who hopes for what is seen? But if we hope for what we do not see, we wait for it with patience.

Likewise the Spirit helps us in our weakness; for we do not know how to pray as we ought, but that very Spirit intercedes with sighs too deep for words. And God, who searches the heart, knows what is the mind of the Spirit, because the Spirit intercedes for the saints according to the will of God.

Psalm 62:1-2

For God alone my soul in silence waits; from him comes my salvation. He alone is my rock and my salvation, my stronghold, so that I shall not be greatly shaken.

Mark 8:22-26

They came to Bethsaida. Some people brought a blind man to him and begged him to touch him. He took the blind man by the hand and led him out of the village; and when he had put saliva on his eyes and laid his hands on him, he asked him, "Can you see anything?" And the man looked up and said, "I can see people, but they look like trees, walking." Then Jesus laid his hands on his eyes again; and he looked intently and his sight was restored, and he saw everything clearly. Then he sent him away to his home, saying, "Do not even go into the village."

SPIRITUAL REFLECTION

A rabbi friend of mine, Darren, tells the story of arriving early to pick his sons up from school and hearing them sing this Spiritual. He was a little taken aback, wondering if the school was trying to make his sons into Christians. He spoke to the teacher who reminded him that we all have a light to shine. He tells me that every Hanukkah, since that time, he and his boys sing this Spiritual.

For the Slaves who walked in the shadows of darkness and death on a daily basis, this Spiritual was their anthem and creed. A powerful song that requires a lot of courage to sing and believe, the words of this Spiritual invite us to be the change and light we want in the world. The words call us into a commitment to do and be something that represents the light of Christ.

This Spiritual is one of the most recognized and sung of the Spirituals. In its simplicity, it communicates a powerful response to the declaration of Jesus who called himself the light of the world. The Civil Rights movement and the Black Lives Matter movement call upon all of us to shine our lights.

"This Little Light of Mine" reminds all of us that we do not have to be great and powerful to have an impact. Sometimes we do not have much or cannot do much, but everybody can do a little. Everybody has a little light.

The Spiritual also calls us to remember the power of darkness in our world. Our call as Christians is to bring light to the darkness. And an essential part of bringing light to any situation is first acknowledging that darkness exists. Sometimes we hesitate to dwell on this fact too much, and we refuse to admit that there are people who strive to maintain the darkness. But spiritual darkness resists the light. And Jesus reminds us that spiritual darkness will never overcome the light.

The determination within the Spiritual requires that we not just sing it but act on it. God calls us to let our light shine. God calls us to shine a light on the evils of poverty, militarism, and racism, (as Dr. Martin Luther King Jr. listed them.)

In the Christian tradition, every person is given a lighted candle at baptism. It is a way of reminding the Christian community that we all have a little light. It is God in us. It is the Source of truth that compels us to shine justice like a light. May we remember to let our light shine as a way to dispel the darkness of poverty and racism. To shine our little light is to be the presence of Christ in the world today.

SPIRITUAL COMMITMENT

- Reread the Spiritual. What are you being called to do with your little light?

- Spend some time reading Dr. King's "I Have a Dream" speech or some of the writings of James Baldwin on race matters.

- How do these scriptures invite you to see and think differently about poverty, militarism, and racism?

- What light can you shine on race relations today, in terms of how your life interacts with the lives of others?

- What do these scriptures have to teach us about a Christian response to places and people in the world lacking the light of truth and justice?

Just Because

You say you will not deny, betray,
Or sell us out
And you have read books by Black
Authors and you have come out
You have not learned much and of such
We will spit you out of our mouths
Joining the protest with that radical
Sign
Reading Martin Luther Jr. don't
make you a friend of mine
And that you gave him money when
He was broke
That anti-racism class you took don't
Make you woke
Your certificate and your proof of honors
Don't declare that you will give up your
Powers
Posting, reposting,
Hash-tagging, parading
At rallies, even your writings—
Did I break your white heart?
If you don't give your life
There is no cure for your
Ignorance
Privilege
And Racism
Just because

Daniel Saw the Stone

Daniel saw the stone
Rolling down to Babylon.
Daniel saw the stone
Rolling down to Babylon.

It was a great stone
Rolling down to Babylon.
Daniel saw the stone
Rolling down to Babylon.

SCRIPTURE
1 Corinthians 10:23-33

"All things are lawful," but not all things are beneficial. "All things are lawful," but not all things build up. Do not seek your own advantage, but that of the other. Eat whatever is sold in the meat market without raising any question on the ground of conscience, for "the earth and its fullness are the Lord's." If an unbeliever invites you to a meal and you are disposed to go, eat whatever is set before you without raising any question on the ground of conscience. But if someone says to you, "This has been offered in sacrifice," then do not eat it, out of consideration for the one who informed you, and for the sake of conscience—I mean the other's conscience, not your own. For why should my liberty be subject to the judgment of someone else's conscience? If I partake with thankfulness, why should I be denounced because of that for which I give thanks? So, whether you eat or drink, or whatever you do, do everything for the glory of God. Give no offense to Jews or to

Greeks or to the church of God, just as I try to please everyone in everything I do, not seeking my own advantage, but that of many, so that they may be saved.

Psalm 62:3-5

How long will you assail me to crush me, all of you together, as if you were a leaning fence, a toppling wall? They seek only to bring me down from my place of honor; lies are their chief delight. They bless with their lips, but in their hearts they curse.

Mark 9:33-41

Then they came to Capernaum; and when he was in the house he asked them, "What were you arguing about on the way?" But they were silent, for on the way they had argued with one another who was the greatest. He sat down, called the twelve, and said to them, "Whoever wants to be first must be last of all and servant of all." Then he took a little child and put it among them; and taking it in his arms, he said to them, "Whoever welcomes one such child in my name welcomes me, and whoever welcomes me welcomes not me but the one who sent me."

John said to him, "Teacher, we saw someone casting out demons in your name, and we tried to stop him, because he was not following us." But Jesus said, "Do not stop him; for no one who does a deed of power in my name will be able soon afterward to speak evil of me. Whoever is not against us is for us. For truly I tell you, whoever gives you a cup of water to drink because you bear the name of Christ will by no means lose the reward.

SPIRITUAL REFLECTION

For the Slaves and people who experience oppression, the prophets of the Old Testament hold a special place. In the prophets, we see the words and will of God directed against individuals or systems that cause bondage, suffering, or oppression. Prophets in the Bible proclaim the "way of the Lord," and it is always a way of justice, freedom, peace, and life. Prophets who suffer and are killed for their prophecy hold a special place in the life of believers.

Daniel is remembered fondly because he was not afraid to speak truth to power and not afraid to worship the true God. The feats and prophecies of Daniel are legendary, and his experience in the lions' den mirrors somewhat the experiences of the Slaves. When Daniel meets with King Nebuchadnezzar, he tells the king that his kingdom will be destroyed. In this sense, Daniel represents the prophet in every generation who foretells the end to oppressive and unjust regimes. The Slaves saw themselves in Daniel and in his three friends who were thrown into the fiery furnace; their experience of being saved by God gave the Slaves hope and solace.

On many levels, when demonstrators call out for peace and justice for a marginalized group, they are, at the same time, professing a desire to save the dominant group from destruction as well. Black Lives Matter is a call for America to save itself from the sin of racism and the death it brings. There is a prophetic element to the rallying cries of the Black Lives Matter movement; they are, in essence, pointing out the inevitable: "a stone is rolling down to Babylon."

Daniel saw the stone. This Spiritual captures the spirit of the great prophet Daniel in his role as seer and interpreter of dreams. Daniel interprets the dream of the king and tells him that a stone will come and crush the evil that exists in his kingdom. The stone in Daniel's dream represents an overwhelming force and power that will crush the vestiges of power in a society not aligned with God.

Again, for the Slaves, Babylon was a representative city. It represented all forms of organized oppression. The Slaves took great interest in the Bible, especially the passages that showed evil systems being defeated.

The Spiritual sends out a warning by saying "Daniel saw the stone" and asks the singer and hearer, by extension, if they have seen it. If they have not seen the stone, the next question is, how could they miss it? What prevents them from seeing?

The stone is rolling down to Babylon, and it is a great big stone. The stone will obliterate slavery and its legacy of racism. Implicit in the Spiritual is a warning, like that given by Daniel. But there is hope if we can sharpen our seeing—and change and repent from the sins of racism.

SPIRITUAL COMMITMENT

- Reread the Spiritual. What, in your view, does the stone rolling toward Babylon signify today?

- How do the scriptures invite you to be more prophetic in the spirit of Jesus Christ?

- Write a letter to your family or church community inviting them to deepen their commitment to act on behalf of social justice.

- Spend some time in prayer reflecting on how you can be a prophetic voice in confronting racial injustice.

- What does Babylon signify in America today?

Swing Low, Sweet Chariot

Swing low, sweet chariot.
Swing low, sweet chariot.
Coming forth to carry me home.
Swing low, sweet chariot.
Swing low, sweet chariot.
Coming forth to carry me home.

I looked over Jordan,
What did I see?
A band of angels
Coming after me,
Coming forth to carry me home.
Swing low, sweet chariot.

SCRIPTURE
1 Corinthians 13:1-13

If I speak in the tongues of mortals and of angels, but do not have love, I am a noisy gong or a clanging cymbal. And if I have prophetic powers, and understand all mysteries and all knowledge, and if I have all faith, so as to remove mountains, but do not have love, I am nothing. If I give away all my possessions, and if I hand over my body so that I may boast, but do not have love, I gain nothing.

Love is patient; love is kind; love is not envious or boastful or arrogant or rude. It does not insist on its own way; it is not irritable or resentful; it does not rejoice in wrongdoing, but rejoices in the truth. It bears all things, believes all things, hopes all things, endures all things.

Love never ends. But as for prophecies, they will come to an end; as for tongues, they will cease; as for knowledge, it will come to an end. For we know only in part, and we prophesy only in part; but when the complete comes, the partial will come to an end. When I was a child, I spoke like a child, I thought like a child, I reasoned like a child; when I became an adult, I put an end to childish ways. For now we see in a mirror, dimly, but then we will see face to face. Now I know only in part; then I will know fully, even as I have been fully known. And now faith, hope, and love abide, these three; and the greatest of these is love.

Psalm 62:6-9

For God alone my soul in silence waits; truly, my hope is in him. He alone is my rock and my salvation, my stronghold, so that I shall not be shaken. In God is my safety and my honor; God is my strong rock and my refuge. Put your trust in him always, O people, pour out your hearts before him, for God is our refuge.

Mark 10:46-52

They came to Jericho. As he and his disciples and a large crowd were leaving Jericho, Bartimaeus son of Timaeus, a blind beggar, was sitting by the roadside. When he heard that it was Jesus of Nazareth, he began to shout out and say, "Jesus, Son of David, have mercy on me!" Many sternly ordered him to be quiet, but he cried out even more loudly, "Son of David, have mercy on me!" Jesus stood still and said, "Call him here." And they called the blind man, saying to him, "Take heart; get up, he is calling you." So throwing off his cloak, he sprang up and came to Jesus. Then Jesus said to him, "What do you want me to do for you?" The blind man said to him, "My teacher, let me see again." Jesus said to him, "Go; your faith has made you well." Immediately he regained his sight and followed him on the way.

SPIRITUAL REFLECTION

Throughout the Bible, there is mention of God as helper, and many stories show us the importance of helping each other. There is no denying that we exist to be of help to each other. Jesus goes as far as to say that when we are present to folks in need, we are present to him. We are called to be good Samaritans on life's journey. To be human is to experience moments when we need to rely on the goodness of others. Hopefully, in those moments, we are reminded that we should pay it forward, doing for others the good that has been done to us.

The Black Lives Matter movement seeks to call attention to the injustice of racism that causes so many African Americans to be abused and killed by the police. Oftentimes, people in the African American communities see a lack of accountability by the police. Officers are acquitted by courts and often allowed to continue working, even when the crime is obvious and public. "We want justice now" is one of the chants one hears at the rallies organized by the Black Lives Matter movement. Now is the time for justice.

"Swing Low, Sweet Chariot" speaks to the depths of desperation felt by many in the Slave population. They were treated like animals and regulated to live in subhuman conditions, a requirement of the institution of slavery. Slave manuals declared that Slaves were lower than farm animals.

No matter the degradation, the Slaves never lost sense of their personal dignity nor their faith in a God who would swing low to redeem them. Oftentimes, it is human nature to cling to hope, no matter how low and bitter one's reality is. The Slaves believed that God was the one who would never forget them. And so they clung to God. God would swing low for them; God would not abandon them.

The Jordan River holds great significance in the scriptures. In its water many were healed, many found their livelihoods, and, in it, Jesus was baptized. For Slaves, the Jordan River offered them hope that they would experience new life.

The prophet Elijah was carried away in a chariot of fire, and the Ethiopian eunuch received salvation while riding in his chariot. "Sweet chariot" refers to the belief in God's salvation and God's promise to take the Slaves home.

The Slaves kept their hope alive and believed that God would rescue them, that God would make a way out of no way. Of course, the Slaves also used their own methods of coding their messages of hope and escape. Within this song was a reminder that "home" meant freedom and that there were angels coming to rescue them, in the form of freedom fighters. "Swing low" often meant be quiet or cautious. "Coming for to carry me home" could mean that help was on the way or that it was your time to break free.

SPIRITUAL COMMITMENT

- Reread the Spiritual. Where do you see hopeful signs in the struggle against racism?

- How do the scriptures challenge you to respond to a culture where people are kept "low"?

- The mention of Jordan invites us to think about our baptismal promises. As we think about the realities of race in America today, what benefits do baptism offer us? Think about your own or your church's core values and notice if there are any similarities to those of the Black Lives Matter movement.

- Think about the angels that have accompanied you on your life journey. Now, think about how you might be an angel or act like an angel in the fight for racial justice.

- Where do you see signs of hope for a world in which each human being is treated as wholly human, whole, and holy?

My Lord, What a Morning

My Lord, what a morning.
My Lord, what a morning.
My Lord, what a morning,
When the stars begin to fall.

My Lord, what a morning.
My Lord, what a morning.
My Lord, what a morning,
When the sun begins to shine.

SCRIPTURE
2 Corinthians 1:3-11

Blessed be the God and Father of our Lord Jesus Christ, the Father of mercies and the God of all consolation, who consoles us in all our affliction, so that we may be able to console those who are in any affliction with the consolation with which we ourselves are consoled by God. For just as the sufferings of Christ are abundant for us, so also our consolation is abundant through Christ. If we are being afflicted, it is for your consolation and salvation; if we are being consoled, it is for your consolation, which you experience when you patiently endure the same sufferings that we are also suffering.

Our hope for you is unshaken; for we know that as you share in our sufferings, so also you share in our consolation. We do not want you to be unaware, brothers and sisters, of the affliction we experienced in Asia; for we were so utterly, unbearably crushed that we despaired of life itself. Indeed, we felt that we had received the sentence of death so that we would rely not on ourselves but on God who raises the dead.

He who rescued us from so deadly a peril will continue to rescue us; on him we have set our hope that he will rescue us again, as you also join in helping us by your prayers, so that many will give thanks on our behalf for the blessing granted us through the prayers of many.

Psalm 71:4-6

Deliver me, my God, from the hand of the wicked, from the clutches of the evildoer and the oppressor. For you are my hope, O Lord GOD, my confidence since I was young. I have been sustained by you ever since I was born; from my mother's womb you have been my strength; my praise shall be always of you.

Luke 9:37-45

On the next day, when they had come down from the mountain, a great crowd met him. Just then a man from the crowd shouted, "Teacher, I beg you to look at my son; he is my only child. Suddenly a spirit seizes him, and all at once he shrieks. It convulses him until he foams at the mouth; it mauls him and will scarcely leave him. I begged your disciples to cast it out, but they could not." Jesus answered, "You faithless and perverse generation, how much longer must I be with you and bear with you? Bring your son here." While he was coming, the demon dashed him to the ground in convulsions. But Jesus rebuked the unclean spirit, healed the boy, and gave him back to his father.

And all were astounded at the greatness of God. While everyone was amazed at all that he was doing, he said to his disciples, "Let these words sink into your ears: The Son of Man is going to be betrayed into human hands." But they did not understand this saying; its meaning was concealed from them, so that they could not perceive it. And they were afraid to ask him about this saying.

SPIRITUAL REFLECTION

In the language of recovery, there is often use of the term "rock bottom." It refers to an experience of such loss, desperation, suffering, and betrayal that one cannot but go up from the experience. At times, it is only when we have lost everything that we realize what we truly need. Sometimes, we have to see the tragic reality, the rock bottom of our situation before we seek help or cry for help. Slavery was, without a doubt, a rock-bottom experience for humanity—but it was masterfully concealed from the rest of society. Visits to plantations were carefully calculated to present a picture of grand Southern life, and even to this day there exists misinformation. For instance, some claim, inaccurately, that life as a Slave was better than the life the Africans had in Africa.

It is said that the images of police brutality—the hoses turned on African Americans and dogs biting demonstrators—helped to turn public opinion against the segregation laws primarily based in the southern states of America.

"What a Morning" is a way of highlighting extraordinary events of a new day. Extraordinary events, as we know, can be beautiful or they can be horrendous. What a morning when the Slaves in the Americas saw more and more Africans arriving. What a morning when they saw families being separated, mothers crying as their children were ripped from them. What a morning when they witnessed the arbitrary cruel and excessive punishments meted out to their fellow Slaves. What a morning when they saw some Slaves try to escape, get recaptured, or be killed in the act of escaping. What a morning when a Slave woman bore a slave master's child or was forced to bear multiple children to work in the fields.

What a morning to hear the news about Trayvon Martin. What a morning to hear the news about Breonna Taylor. What a morning to see the video of George Floyd dying under the knee of the police officer for more than nine minutes.

Stars falling, under any circumstances, would be considered a phenomenon. There is no denying that we can become immune to or blissfully unaware of profound or extraordinary happenings. For instance, many people miss the sunrise or the sunset; sometimes they just do not even notice.

It is difficult to imagine how the traumatic horrors of slavery and racism can be ignored or missed in American society. This Spiritual invites the listener to pay attention to painful reality and to ponder a day when the second meaning of extraordinary as something to marvel at comes into view and takes root. What a time we live in today. What a morning we live in today. My Lord, what an extraordinary morning you have promised.

SPIRITUAL COMMITMENT

- Reread the Spiritual. What feelings come up for you as you watch televised acts of police brutality?

- How do the scriptures invite you to think differently about police brutality or to be more prophetic in the spirit of Jesus Christ?

- Write a letter to your family or church community sharing your thoughts about Trayvon Martin, Breonna Taylor, and/or George Floyd.

- Spend some time in prayer reflecting on what actions you could take as a means of confronting racial injustice.

- What do the lines "when the stars begin to fall" and "the sun begins to shine" mean to you?

Is There Anybody Here Who Loves My Jesus?

Is there anybody here who loves my Jesus?
Is there anybody here who loves my Jesus?
I want to know if you love my Jesus,
I want to know if you love my Lord.

This world's a wilderness of woe,
So let us all to glory go.
Religion is a blooming rose,
And none but them who feel it knows.

When I was blind and could not see,
King Jesus brought the light to me.
When every star refuses to shine,
I know King Jesus will be mine.

SCRIPTURE
Galatians 4:21-31

Tell me, you who desire to be subject to the law, will you not listen to the law? For it is written that Abraham had two sons, one by a slave woman and the other by a free woman. One, the child of the slave, was born according to the flesh; the other, the child of the free woman, was born through the promise. Now this is an allegory: these women are two covenants. One woman, in fact, is Hagar, from Mount Sinai, bearing children for slavery. Now Hagar is Mount Sinai in Arabia and corresponds to the present Jerusalem, for she is in slavery with her children. But the other woman corresponds to the Jerusalem above; she is free, and she is our mother. For it is written, "Rejoice, you childless one, you who bear no children, burst into song and shout, you who endure no birthpangs;

for the children of the desolate woman are more numerous than the children of the one who is married." Now you, my friends, are children of the promise, like Isaac. But just as at that time the child who was born according to the flesh persecuted the child who was born according to the Spirit, so it is now also. But what does the scripture say? "Drive out the slave and her child; for the child of the slave will not share the inheritance with the child of the free woman." So then, friends, we are children, not of the slave but of the free woman.

Psalm 77:4-6

You will not let my eyelids close; I am troubled and I cannot speak. I consider the days of old; I remember the years long past; I commune with my heart in the night; I ponder and search my mind.

Luke 10:1-12

After this the Lord appointed seventy others and sent them on ahead of him in pairs to every town and place where he himself intended to go. He said to them, "The harvest is plentiful, but the laborers are few; therefore ask the Lord of the harvest to send out laborers into his harvest. Go on your way. See, I am sending you out like lambs into the midst of wolves. Carry no purse, no bag, no sandals; and greet no one on the road. Whatever house you enter, first say, 'Peace to this house!' And if anyone is there who shares in peace, your peace will rest on that person; but if not, it will return to you. Remain in the same house, eating and drinking whatever they provide, for the laborer deserves to be paid. Do not move about from house to house. Whenever you enter a town and its people welcome you, eat what is set before you; cure the sick who are there, and say to them, 'The kingdom of God has come near to you.' But whenever you enter a town and they do not welcome you, go out into its streets and say, 'Even the dust of your town that clings to our feet, we wipe off in protest against you. Yet know this: the kingdom of God has come near.' I tell you, on that day it will be more tolerable for Sodom than for that town.

SPIRITUAL REFLECTION

Do you love me? This is the most important question of all. Even Jesus asks it. Jesus asks this question to Peter, the one who signifies the faith of the church, all believers. *Do you love me?* Peter declares rightly that Jesus knows everything and knows he loves him. This truth does not prevent Jesus from asking the question in the first place.

All human beings are created in love, to love, and be loved. Everything, everyone, and all that is, all things are created by the God who is love. Love and all that it embodies—especially its commitment to living a life of respect for all, care for the vulnerable, and a commitment to the golden rule—requires that we speak and act in and with love. Love requires a commitment on our part to talk the talk and walk the walk.

The Slaves in America knew the hatred of their masters and the system of slavery. Only hate could have fueled and kept ablaze such a monument of dehumanization, a cruel sin of unparalleled proportions. Slavery is the embodiment of the Antichrist, because it is so anti-love.

When the Slaves sang this Spiritual, they gave voice to the very voice of Jesus Christ who felt abandoned on the cross. *Is there anybody here who loves my Jesus?* This is the question of those who suffer, inviting us to recall that it is Jesus Christ who said what you do to the least you do to me. How did the Christian church hear, interpret, and live a belief in Jesus, the embodiment of God's Love?

African Americans today ask all Americans, especially Christians: is there anybody here who loves my Jesus? Dr. Martin Luther King Jr. linked racism with poverty and militarism as the three major sins of America. African Americans encounter the sins of racism and poverty daily, because America refuses to share the fruits, which are requirements of true repentance. The brutality, disrespect, neglect, and death experienced by many in the African

American community come directly from a racism that lives on from the time of slavery.

Is there anybody here who loves my Jesus? I want to know if you love my Jesus. I want to know... For those of us who commit to loving our neighbor as ourselves, we commit to living like Jesus. That Jesus loves us and the whole world is one of the earliest Christian truths we learn as children. Just as we sing that Jesus loves all the children of the world, we too are called to love everyone, especially the victims of racism. To love Jesus requires some undeniable actions and responses on our part. To love Jesus calls us to renounce slavery, its consequences, and all manifestations of the systemic racism that survives today. Our call as Christians is to love Jesus and to show that love in undeniable actions of love.

SPIRITUAL COMMITMENT

- Reread the Spiritual. How would you answer the question being asked by the Spiritual? How would members of your family and church answer the question?

- What do the scriptures have to say to you about loving God and your neighbor as yourself?

- There is no denying that as children of God we are all being sent out to love. What is the good news that Jesus is sending you out to speak and do?

- Think about ways you are called to love Jesus today.

- Where do you see signs of love of neighbor in your neighborhood?

Every Time, I Feel the Spirit

Every time, I feel the Spirit
Moving in my heart, I pray.
Every time, I feel the Spirit
Moving in my heart, I pray.

Upon the mountain my Lord spoke.
Out of his mouth came fire and smoke.
Looked all around me, it looked so fine,
And the Lord said, it was all mine.
Jordan River is chilly and cold.
It chills the body but not the soul.
There is just one train, upon this track.
It runs to heaven and runs right back.

Every time, I feel the Spirit
Moving in my heart, I pray.
Every time, I feel the Spirit
Moving in my heart, I pray.

SCRIPTURE
Ephesians 3:7-17

Of this gospel I have become a servant according to the gift of God's grace that was given me by the working of his power. Although I am the very least of all the saints, this grace was given to me to bring to the Gentiles the news of the boundless riches of Christ, and to make everyone see what is the plan of the mystery hidden for ages in God who created all things; so that through the church the wisdom of God in its rich variety might now be made known to the rulers and authorities in the heavenly places. This was in accordance with the eternal purpose that he has carried out in Christ Jesus our Lord, in whom we have access to God in boldness and confidence through faith in him. I pray therefore that you may not lose heart over my sufferings for you; they are your glory.

For this reason I bow my knees before the Father, from whom every family in heaven and on earth takes its name. I pray that, according to the riches of his glory, he may grant that you may be strengthened in your inner being with power through his Spirit, and that Christ may dwell in your hearts through faith, as you are being rooted and grounded in love.

Psalm 81: 11-14

And yet my people did not hear my voice, and Israel would not obey me. So I gave them over to the stubbornness of their hearts, to follow their own devices. Oh, that my people would listen to me! that Israel would walk in my ways! I should soon subdue their enemies and turn my hand against their foes.

Luke 12:13-21

Someone in the crowd said to him, "Teacher, tell my brother to divide the family inheritance with me." But he said to him, "Friend, who set me to be a judge or arbitrator over you?" And he said to them, "Take care! Be on your guard against all kinds of greed; for one's life does not consist in the abundance of possessions." Then he told them a parable: "The land of a rich man produced abundantly. And he thought to himself, 'What should I do, for I have no place to store my crops?' Then he said, 'I will do this: I will pull down my barns and build larger ones, and there I will store all my grain and my goods. And I will say to my soul, 'Soul, you have ample goods laid up for many years; relax, eat, drink, be merry.' But God said to him, 'You fool! This very night your life is being demanded of you. And the things you have prepared, whose will they be?' So it is with those who store up treasures for themselves but are not rich toward God."

SPIRITUAL REFLECTION

Every time, I feel the Spirit moving in my heart, I pray. President Obama said to the author Ta-Nehisi Coates that one should never give in to despair. Hope is one of the most powerful virtues we receive from the Holy Spirit. Another way of saying this is to affirm a belief in humanity's natural bending toward hope: hope is a human value; to live is to have hope.

When the Slaves sang about feeling the Spirit and prayer, they were reminding each other to keep hope alive. To feel the Spirit reminded the Slaves that God had never forsaken them—and will never. At the heart of the Slaves' true faith in God was a commitment to a faithfulness. Slavery was interpreted by the spiritual leadership among the Slaves as akin to being enslaved in Egypt. Knowing that story gave them confidence in their liberation—and they knew they had to be a part of their future liberation. Being a Christian meant an experience of the cross, and slavery demonstrated the deepest fulfillment of the cross. All the experiences of Jesus's life—betrayal, denial, condemnation, crucifixion, death, and resurrection—would have to happen in the lives of those most committed to God.

Feeling the Spirit in the heart reminded the Slaves not to give in to despair: they remembered the Lord who spoke on the mountain to Moses and prophets. All the biblical stories of imprisonment mattered to the Slaves; they knew them and believed them. The Slaves experienced God as Liberator during the most miserable day in slavery. We do great harm to the memory of the faith of the Slaves if we do not believe that they kept their faith and gathered inspiration from it.

Singing the Lord's songs in a strange land is what followers of God have to do. The scripture readings for today speak to living into the awareness of faithfulness in the face of suffering.

As Christians today we are called to live the word of the Lord, which is to love God and our neighbor as ourselves. To pray as a

Christian is to commit to actions of liberation and freedom. This is what it means not to give into despair. To pray is to believe, and to believe is to put one's heart into hope. To live with hope today requires us to stand up for justice and peace. We are called to march and do what we can to stomp out despair.

When we feel the Spirit, we must obey the Spirit. The Spirit calls us to live in the now, to live knowing that we are called to do what we need to do today: speak truth to power, endure the present suffering trying our best not to lose hope, and stay in reality and truth while believing in the resurrection.

To be people of faith is to live the now the way Jesus lived. We must be channels of God's peace, couriers of the good news to the poor, and agents of liberation. It is what we are called to do and be; it is one of the important messages we hear and learn from the Spiritual.

SPIRITUAL COMMITMENT

- Reread the Spiritual. How and what does this Spiritual move in your heart?

- What do the scriptures have to say to you about how you pray and what prayer means to you?

- How do you persevere today and not lose hope or fall into despair?

- Think about ways you are called to resist despair.

- Consider these words from the Spiritual: "Jordan River is chilly and cold. It chills the body but not the soul." What do these words mean to you?

Deep River

Deep river, my home is over Jordan.
Deep river, Lord, I want to cross over to camp ground.
Oh don't you want to go to that gospel feast.
That promised land where all is peace?

Oh deep river, Lord, I want to cross over to camp ground.

SCRIPTURE
Philippians 2:1-11

If then there is any encouragement in Christ, any consolation from love, any sharing in the Spirit, any compassion and sympathy, make my joy complete: be of the same mind, having the same love, being in full accord and of one mind. Do nothing from selfish ambition or conceit, but in humility regard others as better than yourselves. Let each of you look not to your own interests, but to the interests of others. Let the same mind be in you that was in Christ Jesus, who, though he was in the form of God, did not regard equality with God as something to be exploited, but emptied himself, taking the form of a slave, being born in human likeness. And being found in human form, he humbled himself and became obedient to the point of death—even death on a cross. Therefore God also highly exalted him and gave him the name that is above every name, so that at the name of Jesus every knee should bend, in heaven and on earth and under the earth, and every tongue should confess that Jesus Christ is Lord, to the glory of God the Father.

Psalm 84:9-12

For one day in your courts is better than a thousand in my own room, and to stand at the threshold of the house of my God than to dwell in the tents of the wicked. For the LORD God is both sun and shield; he will give grace and glory; No good thing will the LORD withhold from those who walk with integrity. O LORD of hosts, happy are they who put their trust in you!

Luke 13:10-17

Now he was teaching in one of the synagogues on the sabbath. And just then there appeared a woman with a spirit that had crippled her for eighteen years. She was bent over and was quite unable to stand up straight. When Jesus saw her, he called her over and said, "Woman, you are set free from your ailment." When he laid his hands on her, immediately she stood up straight and began praising God. But the leader of the synagogue, indignant because Jesus had cured on the sabbath, kept saying to the crowd, "There are six days on which work ought to be done; come on those days and be cured, and not on the sabbath day." But the Lord answered him and said, "You hypocrites! Does not each of you on the sabbath untie his ox or his donkey from the manger, and lead it away to give it water? And ought not this woman, a daughter of Abraham whom Satan bound for eighteen long years, be set free from this bondage on the sabbath day?" When he said this, all his opponents were put to shame; and the entire crowd was rejoicing at all the wonderful things that he was doing.

SPIRITUAL REFLECTION

With a history of four hundred years of slavery in America, no one should expect that the effects of slavery will simply disappear overnight. The generations of those who lived through the experience of slavery are marked deeply and forever. But descendants of Slaves hold a legacy of ongoing commitment to freedom and thriving, no matter the challenges of the present day. To live in freedom and to thrive requires an acknowledgement and affirmation of the deep anger, division, alienation, and suffering caused by the sustained attitudes and activities in slavery.

The Spirituals have long given witness to the indomitable faith of the Slaves in what was a most challenging time in their life. We remember the millions of Slaves who never experienced freedom, dying decades or centuries before slavery ended. What must it have been like for Slaves to keep believing in the promises of God while enduring the harsh cruelty of slavery? When we are tested and when we are suffering, we might draw encouragement from the Slaves who somehow managed to remain faithful to their hope and dream that one day they would be free.

Deep river, my home is over Jordan. For the Slaves, knowledge of the Jordan River was an important place marker in their understanding of their faith and the Bible. For Jews as well as Christians, the Jordan River holds major significance because the Israelites crossed it to enter the Promised Land and because Jesus was baptized in it by John the Baptist. The crossing into freedom and the baptism of Jesus assured the Slaves that they would one day be free and in Jesus they could experience God saying to them, "These are my beloved children, in whom I am well pleased."

It is said that in order to achieve something in its fullness, one has to be able to visualize it and maintain the desired object in one's consciousness. The deep river signified for the Slaves the danger, the horror, the death-dealing drowning effects of slavery, and, at the same time, it signified for them something they needed to get through, to endure. Of course, the fact that Jesus was baptized in the Jordan River gave them great comfort, because it further symbolized that they needed to get through the waters of the Jordan and experience a rebirth. They believed that they would one day be born again into something new and powerful: a freedom that was guaranteed in God.

Oh, don't you want to go to that gospel feast, that promised land where all is peace? Oh, deep river, Lord, I want to cross over to camp ground. African Americans, today, still make this their song, a kind of mantra, a vow. All of us people of goodwill and baptized in the Jordan along with Christ commit to doing all that we can to ensure we live in the "gospel feast, that promised land" now. This is the fulfillment of our baptismal vows and promises: to work for the dignity, freedom, and respect for all our brothers and sisters. Holding an image of the River Jordan, we commit to a belief that advocates the dismantling, abolishing, and rethinking of religion, culture, and any institution that supports enslavement and racism.

SPIRITUAL COMMITMENT

- Reread the Spiritual. What effects of racism still run deeply in American culture today?

- What do the scriptures have to say to you about how the church should respond to institutionalized racism?

- Spend some time reflecting on your baptism. What is the good news you experience from your baptism as you reflect on this Spiritual?

- Have a conversation with a friend or family member about countering racism in America with hope and endurance.

- Where can you have an impact in the area of race relations?

Surely He Died on Calvary

Calvary, Calvary, Calvary, Calvary, Calvary,
Calvary, surely he died on Calvary.

Every time I think about Jesus,
Every time I think about Jesus,
Every time I think about Jesus,
Surely he died on Calvary.

Don't you hear the hammering?
Don't you hear the hammering?
Don't you hear the hammering?
Surely he died on Calvary.

Don't you hear him calling his mother?
Don't you hear him calling his Father?
Don't you hear him calling his Father?
Surely he died on Calvary.

SCRIPTURE
Colossians 2:6-15

As you therefore have received Christ Jesus the Lord, continue to live your lives in him, rooted and built up in him and established in the faith, just as you were taught, abounding in thanksgiving. See to it that no one takes you captive through philosophy and empty deceit, according to human tradition, according to the elemental spirits of the universe, and not according to Christ. For in him the whole fullness of deity dwells bodily, and you have come to fullness in him, who is the head of every ruler and authority. In him also you were circumcised with a spiritual circumcision, by putting off the body of the flesh in the circumcision of Christ; when you were buried with him in baptism, you were also raised with him through faith in the power of God, who raised him from the dead.

And when you were dead in trespasses and the uncircumcision of your flesh, God made you alive together with him, when he forgave us all our trespasses, erasing the record that stood against us with its legal demands. He set this aside, nailing it to the cross. He disarmed the rulers and authorities and made a public example of them, triumphing over them in it.

Psalm 86:1-3

Bow down your ear, O LORD, and answer me, for I am poor and in misery. Keep watch over my life, for I am faithful; save your servant who puts his trust in you. Be merciful to me, O LORD, for you are my God; I call upon you all the day long.

Luke 14:25-33

Now large crowds were traveling with him; and he turned and said to them, "Whoever comes to me and does not hate father and mother, wife and children, brothers and sisters, yes, and even life itself, cannot be my disciple. Whoever does not carry the cross and follow me cannot be my disciple. For which of you, intending to build a tower, does not first sit down and estimate the cost, to see whether he has enough to complete it? Otherwise, when he has laid a foundation and is not able to finish, all who see it will begin to ridicule him, saying, 'This fellow began to build and was not able to finish.' Or what king, going out to wage war against another king, will not sit down first and consider whether he is able with ten thousand to oppose the one who comes against him with twenty thousand? If he cannot, then, while the other is still far away, he sends a delegation and asks for the terms of peace. So therefore, none of you can become my disciple if you do not give up all your possessions.

SPIRITUAL REFLECTION

African Americans in Christian communities have long paid special attention to the suffering and death of Jesus as a lens through which they could view their own experience. Calvary, for African Americans, is more than a place; it is a state of mind and a current reality.

Think of all the African American parents who have the talk with their children about how to conduct themselves on the street and in the presence of the police. Think of all the conversations in African American homes where children are warned about where to walk and how to walk. Then think of the children themselves, especially the teenagers, who never feel comfortable in their own skin—never feel safe in their own neighborhoods.

Jesus died on Calvary, and African Americans experience themselves being hunted in the streets and being killed by the very people paid to protect them. For Christians who believe in Jesus Christ, the crucifixion of others must always jar our consciences and remind us that our role is to turn toward—and not to abandon—the suffering other. The story of Calvary is written so that we, as Christians, practice staying with suffering, so that we commit to standing with Mary at the foot of the cross. The Christian message, in truth, proclaims that we must pay attention to the Calvary of others and expose the agents of death.

The targeting can be subtle. Our American society has a penchant for making the poor, the vulnerable, and the African American community invisible—except when these groups provide a way to shore up the myths that the society seeks so hard to present as true.

To think about Jesus is to think about his dying on Calvary. Again, the Slaves sent their masters a powerful message when they sang this Spiritual. It proclaimed first their own identification with the suffering and crucified Christ; it confronted the slave masters, asking why they could not see the Slaves in the crucified Christ.

Don't you hear the hammering? No doubt, this question seeks to address the willful ignorance of the slave masters. The hammering signifies that evidence of the crucifixion could be seen throughout the entire plantation. How could one not notice the human degradation, suffering, and brutality of the system of slavery? And what hardness of heart required a hammer to break down?

The Black Lives Matter movement has extended and amplified the sound of hammering so that it can be heard in the consciousness of the American public. *Don't you hear the hammering? Surely he died on Calvary.*

The last verse holds a special place in this Spiritual as it brings home the message in a most poignant way. *Don't you hear him calling his mother? Don't you hear him calling his Father? Don't you hear him calling his Father? Surely he died on Calvary.* The Spiritual called on the world of slaveholders to recognize the suffering and humanity of the Slaves—the Slaves who called out to the Father, as Jesus did near his death.

SPIRITUAL COMMITMENT

- Reread the Spiritual. Where do you see Calvary in American life and society these days?

- How do the scriptures challenge you to respond to the suffering of others or to be like Jesus Christ?

- Write a letter or poem that illustrates your recognition of the suffering of others in your family or society. Set an intention to be a healing presence.

- Think about how you have experienced Calvary, personally, and how it makes you more compassionate.

- What prevents you from hearing the cries of those who suffer?

Faith Sees

Out of the depths and the night
Within me
captured
raped
beaten, shackled, and sold
None have ever even been able to chain
My Black and shining
Soul
I comprehend because I have lived it
I have seen the sorrowful mysteries of my
People—I know them
Black and comely I have seen God
And the look of God
that look that God gave me
and God fashioned me
To see the dark
To see in the dark—not impossible
Quite possible to see with the dark
Standing in and with and
Through the dark.
Faith.

Give Me Jesus

In the morning when I rise,
In the morning when I rise,
In the morning when I rise,
Give me Jesus.

Give me Jesus, give me Jesus.
You may have the whole world.
Give me Jesus.

Dark midnight was my cry.
Dark midnight was my cry.
Dark midnight was my cry.
Give me Jesus.

O when I come to die,
O when I come to die,
O when I come to die,
Give me Jesus.

SCRIPTURE
1 Thessalonians 2:9-16

You remember our labor and toil, brothers and sisters; we worked night and day, so that we might not burden any of you while we proclaimed to you the gospel of God. You are witnesses, and God also, how pure, upright, and blameless our conduct was toward you believers. As you know, we dealt with each one of you like a father with his children, urging and encouraging you and pleading that you lead a life worthy of God, who calls you into his own kingdom and glory.

We also constantly give thanks to God for this, that when you received the word of God that you heard from us, you accepted it not as a human word but as what it really is, God's word, which is also at work in you believers. For you, brothers and sisters, became imitators of the churches of God in Christ Jesus that are in Judea, for you suffered the same things from your own compatriots as they did from the Jews, who killed both the Lord Jesus and the prophets, and drove us out; they displease God and oppose everyone by hindering us from speaking to the Gentiles so that they may be saved. Thus they have constantly been filling up the measure of their sins; but God's wrath has overtaken them at last.

Psalm 90:13-14

Return, O LORD; how long will you tarry? be gracious to your servants. Satisfy us by your loving-kindness in the morning; so shall we rejoice and be glad all the days of our life.

John 1:1-18

In the beginning was the Word, and the Word was with God, and the Word was God. He was in the beginning with God. All things came into being through him, and without him not one thing came into being. What has come into being in him was life, and the life was the light of all people.

The light shines in the darkness, and the darkness did not overcome it. There was a man sent from God, whose name was John. He came as a witness to testify to the light, so that all might believe through him. He himself was not the light, but he came to testify to the light. The true light, which enlightens everyone, was coming into the world.

He was in the world, and the world came into being through him; yet the world did not know him. He came to what was his own, and his own people did not accept him. But to all who received him, who believed in his name, he gave power to become children of God, who were born, not of blood or of the will of the flesh or of the will of man, but of God. And the Word became flesh and lived among us, and we have seen his glory, the glory as of a father's only son, full of grace and truth.

(John testified to him and cried out, "This was he of whom I said, 'He who comes after me ranks ahead of me because he was before me.'") From his fullness we have all received, grace upon grace. The law indeed was given through Moses; grace and truth came through Jesus Christ. No one has ever seen God. It is God the only Son, who is close to the Father's heart, who has made him known.

SPIRITUAL REFLECTION

What is your most consistent prayer when you pray, alone or in community? What are your spiritual desires? Our spiritual lives are defined by the desires of the heart. So, what we desire in prayer and desire from God speak clearly about our love for God and our love for the world. This is true because our prayer reveals our sense of self, our identity, and intentions.

When Dr. Martin Luther King Jr. prepared people for civil disobedience, he insisted that activists deepen their sense of identity and be clear about their intentions. Following his lead, I like to remind the congregation, wherever I do ministry, that they must always remember who they are and whose they are.

One of the horrors of slavery was the deliberate attempt to erase the identity of the Slaves. The system was designed to deprive the Slaves of any love for self, for Africa, or even human freedom. The practice of dividing families is an example of this deliberate dehumanization. Depriving the Slaves of a sense of self made it easier for the slave masters to justify the sinful system of slavery. Slavery demanded the total control of the Black people by reinforcing they were only worthy of slavery and better off as Slaves.

Great efforts were employed to misinform about life in Africa. The slave masters told the Slaves that Africa was vile, uncivilized, primitive, and had nothing of value. As part of this miseducation, the slave masters taught that God had ordained that the Slaves be enslaved. Because of such lies, the Slaves were taught to hate freedom. Seeking their freedom was a sin against God, they were told, and they should seek to remain faithful to their masters, showing their love by working harder.

In light of all this, the Slaves' capacity to trust in God and maintain a faith that God desired their flourishing is beyond extraordinary. Imagine a faith in God so strong that, in the midst of all the suffering and cruelty experienced, a desire for Jesus remains and deepens. The faith of the Slaves must never be underestimated.

In the morning when I rise, give me Jesus. Would to God that we all had faith like these Slaves. Many of the religious leaders in the Civil Rights movement attributed their courage and witness to a profound sense of having Jesus with them. Many said that their quiet prayer time with God in the mornings helped shore up their courage. By desiring Jesus, they could desire justice. Many who do the work of justice and peace today discover that their courage and commitment strengthen when they can say, from the very core of their being: *Give me Jesus, give me Jesus. You may have the whole world, give me Jesus. Oh when I come to die, give me Jesus.*

SPIRITUAL COMMITMENT

- Reread the Spiritual. What are you seeking from God? What do you long for?

- How do you prepare yourself for challenging moments in your spiritual life?

- How do these scriptures invite you to think differently about justice, freedom, and peace?

- What are the essential elements of your spiritual life?

- Do you think you can say/pray: "You may have the whole world, give me Jesus?"

Down by the Riverside

I'm gonna lay down my burden, down by the riverside,
Down by the riverside, down by the riverside.
I'm gonna lay down my burden, down by the riverside.
And I ain't gonna study war no more,
I ain't gonna study war no more.

I'm gonna lay down my sword and shield,
    down by the riverside,
Down by the riverside, down by the riverside.
I'm gonna lay down my sword and shield,
    down by the riverside,
And I ain't gonna study war no more.
I ain't gonna study war no more.

I'm gonna put on my long white robe,
    down by the riverside,
Down by the riverside, down by the riverside.
I'm gonna put on my long white robe,
    down by the riverside,
Down by the riverside, down by the riverside.
I ain't gonna study war no more.

SCRIPTURE
2 Thessalonians 2:5-12

Do you not remember that I told you these things when I was
still with you? And you know what is now restraining him, so
that he may be revealed when his time comes. For the mystery
of lawlessness is already at work, but only until the one who
now restrains it is removed. And then the lawless one will be
revealed, whom the Lord Jesus will destroy with the breath
of his mouth, annihilating him by the manifestation of his

coming. The coming of the lawless one is apparent in the working of Satan, who uses all power, signs, lying wonders, and every kind of wicked deception for those who are perishing, because they refused to love the truth and so be saved. For this reason God sends them a powerful delusion, leading them to believe what is false, so that all who have not believed the truth but took pleasure in unrighteousness will be condemned.

Psalm 91:1-2

He who dwells in the shelter of the Most High, abides under the shadow of the Almighty. He shall say to the LORD, "You are my refuge and my stronghold, my God in whom I put my trust."

John 5:39-47

"You search the scriptures because you think that in them you have eternal life; and it is they that testify on my behalf. Yet you refuse to come to me to have life. I do not accept glory from human beings. But I know that you do not have the love of God in you. I have come in my Father's name, and you do not accept me; if another comes in his own name, you will accept him. How can you believe when you accept glory from one another and do not seek the glory that comes from the one who alone is God? Do not think that I will accuse you before the Father; your accuser is Moses, on whom you have set your hope. If you believed Moses, you would believe me, for he wrote about me. But if you do not believe what he wrote, how will you believe what I say?"

SPIRITUAL REFLECTION

The words, "I'm gonna lay down my burden, down by the riverside," speak to an unshakeable faith and trust in the God of justice, mercy, and divine deliverance. The Slaves understood deeply God's nature as the One who participates in the salvation of humanity, the One who wants all human beings to have life and life more abundantly. God was the One at whose feet they could lay down their burdens and believe in God's deliverance. This Spiritual echoed an ongoing commitment to the God of salvation, who calls all of us to keep heart and to cast our burdens on God.

I ain't gonna study war no more. The presence of faith leaders at the forefront of the Civil Rights movement must never be taken for granted. Of course, many of these leaders did not feel the support of their wider denominational leadership, but they pressed on in their belief that God was calling them to fight for justice. The Civil Rights leaders advocated a commitment to fighting for justice using peaceful means. Indeed, the mantra for all the protests could have been this Spiritual: *I ain't gonna study war no more.*

Throughout every struggle for justice, the question of taking up arms or leading a violent revolution always arises. What do you, the reader, think about the place of violence in religious activism? Dr. Martin Luther King Jr. and the religious leaders of the Civil Rights movement insisted that those who marched with them put aside their sword and shield.

To watch the courage of African Americans integrating schools, integrating restaurants, and marching for justice demonstrates with undeniable clarity their belief in justice and the righteousness of God. They were spat upon, hit with rocks, fired upon, attacked by the police, attacked by police dogs, knocked over with firehoses, beaten, imprisoned, and killed.

In the midst of all their sufferings, the Slaves did not lose sight of their "long white robe." This is a clear reference to them owning the power of their baptism and their faith in God's reign, where those who suffered on earth would find rest for their soul and vindication in God. Today, as we reflect on the sin of racism in this country, how we think about our baptism and what it means to be clothed in Christ matters a great deal.

One cannot separate the courage of African Americans in the twentieth century from the courage and faith of the Slaves. We also should not underestimate the faith of the Slaves who identified completely with Jesus Christ who was betrayed, crucified, and killed. In Jesus Christ, they found recognition of their plight and gained a deeper understanding of the ways of God and men. The slave masters' unwillingness to follow the Golden Rule or commandments of God contributed to the Slaves' choice to cast all their cares on God.

SPIRITUAL COMMITMENT

- Reread the Spiritual. Do you think violence ever has a place in protests for justice and peace?

- What do the scriptures have to say to you about suffering, justice, redemption, and how we reject what is right?

- How is the fight for justice today reflected in the baptismal covenant?

- Spend some time today or this week looking at footage of the Civil Rights marches.

- What gives you hope for a more just and peaceful world?

It's Me, O Lord

It's me, it's me, O Lord,
Standing in the need of prayer.
It's me, it's me, O Lord,
Standing in the need of prayer.

Not my brother, not my sister, but it's me, O Lord,
Standing in the need of prayer.
Not my brother, not my sister, but it's me, O Lord,
Standing in the need of prayer.

Not the preacher, not the deacon, but it's me, O Lord,
Standing in the need of prayer.
Not the preacher, not the deacon, but it's me, O Lord,
Standing in the need of prayer.

Not my father, not my mother, but it's me, O Lord,
Standing in the need of prayer.
Not my father, not my mother, but it's me, O Lord,
Standing in the need of prayer.

Not the stranger, not my neighbor, but it's me, O Lord,
Standing in the need of prayer.
Not the stranger, not my neighbor, but it's me, O Lord,
Standing in the need of prayer.

SCRIPTURE
1 Timothy 6:11-19

But as for you, man of God, shun all this; pursue
righteousness, godliness, faith, love, endurance, gentleness.
Fight the good fight of the faith; take hold of the eternal

life, to which you were called and for which you made the good confession in the presence of many witnesses.

In the presence of God, who gives life to all things, and of Christ Jesus, who in his testimony before Pontius Pilate made the good confession, I charge you to keep the commandment without spot or blame until the manifestation of our Lord Jesus Christ, which he will bring about at the right time—he who is the blessed and only Sovereign, the King of kings and Lord of lords. It is he alone who has immortality and dwells in unapproachable light, whom no one has ever seen or can see; to him be honor and eternal dominion. Amen. As for those who in the present age are rich, command them not to be haughty, or to set their hopes on the uncertainty of riches, but rather on God who richly provides us with everything for our enjoyment. They are to do good, to be rich in good works, generous, and ready to share, thus storing up for themselves the treasure of a good foundation for the future, so that they may take hold of the life that really is life.

Psalm 97:10-11

The LORD loves those who hate evil; he preserves the lives of his saints and delivers them from the hand of the wicked. Light has sprung up for the righteous, and joyful gladness for those who are truehearted.

John 6:35-40

Jesus said to them, "I am the bread of life. Whoever comes to me will never be hungry, and whoever believes in me will never be thirsty. But I said to you that you have seen me and yet do not believe. Everything that the Father gives me will come to me, and anyone who comes to me I will never drive away; for I have come down from heaven, not to do my own will, but the will of him who sent me. And this is the will of him who sent me, that I should lose nothing of all that he has given me, but raise it up on the last day. This is indeed the will of my Father, that all who see the Son and believe in him may have eternal life; and I will raise them up on the last day."

SPIRITUAL REFLECTION

It's me, it's me, O Lord, standing in the need of prayer. It's me.
Grammatically, the correct sentence should be "It is I," however, I like "It's me" because the phrase is more colloquial and evokes a sense of intimacy with God. Either way, the Spiritual calls us to a focus on self. This Spiritual also reminds me of Jesus asking his disciples: Who do you say that I am? In the Apostles' Creed, we say that Jesus will come again to judge the living and the dead. Each of us will have to answer for the choices and the actions we support in God's name, for the things we have done and the things we have failed to do.

What does it mean to stand in the need of prayer? Human beings need to come before God in prayer, recognizing our dependence on God. Prayer connects us to our needs and the needs of others as well. But prayer is not always easy. Oftentimes, Christian communities settle for convenient and comfortable truths about God and forget how God seeks to challenge them to a more radical following of Jesus Christ. Prayer is a more revolutionary act than Christians realize because when we pray, we invoke the will of God in our lives and in the world. Prayer requires that we work for justice, seek God's justice, and do all in our power to work for justice and peace.

"Standing in the need of prayer" suggested to the Slave the need for God's assistance, presence and power. The Slaves knew that they were in need of prayer and hoped that their masters understood their roles in providing for their human needs and an end to their misery. Out of the experiences of the Slaves came the searing question: what does it really mean to live as Christians in community? How does one pray in the midst of ceaseless suffering and cruelty?

The Spiritual questions the prayer of the slave masters as well. The Slaves point to the prayer life of the slave masters and the Christian community and ask them to examine the integrity of their own prayer. How does one kneel in prayer and then deny the needs of suffering others?

As the church prays today, we must grow in awareness that prayer is an act in which the love of God and the love of neighbor come to the fore. Of course, prayer takes on deeper meaning when the community lives out its prayer. Each individual must accept the challenge and obligations of prayer.

Not the preacher, not the deacon, but it's me, O Lord, standing in the need of prayer. Not my father, not my mother, but it's me, O Lord. Not the stranger, not my neighbor, but it's me, O Lord, standing in the need of prayer. This Spiritual reminds us of Jesus's words that whatever we do to the least, we do to him. Jesus shows us that he is the presence of God and reassures us that each and every person is the presence and image of the Living God.

SPIRITUAL COMMITMENT

- Reread the Spiritual. How do you pray and what does your prayer reveal about you?

- How do the scriptures invite you to pray in a more radical way and lead you to a deeper commitment to the lives of others?

- Write a letter to your family or church community inviting them to act upon the issues of poverty, racism, or justice in your community.

- How is the African American community in need of prayer?

- How are you in the need of prayer?

This Feeling

Deep
Deep down
in an ancient, delicate, and familiar place of me
There echoes a song that never stops flowing.
O Black Child don't you weep
Don't you moan
Satan Pharaoh Herod Babylon have fallen
And their bridges burning down
These are days when nothing consoles me
When I arrive in
my sanctuary
wanting the whole universe to burn.

Then, when I listen,
I hear
Deep, deep, deep river
Whispering to the sands and rocks
I know I must keep on
flowing
Deep down
From time before time
Created
Embraced
Celebrated
Conjugated
Loved.
To love.

I Want to Be Ready

I want to be ready, I want to be ready.
I want to be ready to walk in Jerusalem
Just like John.

John said that Jerusalem was four square.
Walk in Jerusalem just like John.
I hope, good Lord, I'll meet you there,
Walk in Jerusalem just like John.

When Peter was preaching at Pentecost,
Walk in Jerusalem just like John.
O he was filled with the Holy Ghost,
Walk in Jerusalem just like John.

SCRIPTURE

2 Timothy 2:8-13

Remember Jesus Christ, raised from the dead, a descendant of David—that is my gospel, for which I suffer hardship, even to the point of being chained like a criminal. But the word of God is not chained. Therefore I endure everything for the sake of the elect, so that they may also obtain the salvation that is in Christ Jesus, with eternal glory. The saying is sure: If we have died with him, we will also live with him; if we endure, we will also reign with him; if we deny him, he will also deny us; if we are faithless, he remains faithful—for he cannot deny himself.

Psalm 100:3-4

Enter his gates with thanksgiving; go into his courts with praise; give thanks to him and call upon his Name. For the LORD is good; his mercy is everlasting; and his faithfulness endures from age to age.

John 8:1-11

While Jesus went to the Mount of Olives. Early in the morning he came again to the temple. All the people came to him and he sat down and began to teach them. The scribes and the Pharisees brought a woman who had been caught in adultery; and making her stand before all of them, they said to him, "Teacher, this woman was caught in the very act of committing adultery. Now in the law Moses commanded us to stone such women. Now what do you say?" They said this to test him, so that they might have some charge to bring against him. Jesus bent down and wrote with his finger on the ground. When they kept on questioning him, he straightened up and said to them, "Let anyone among you who is without sin be the first to throw a stone at her." And once again he bent down and wrote on the ground. When they heard it, they went away, one by one, beginning with the elders; and Jesus was left alone with the woman standing before him. Jesus straightened up and said to her, "Woman, where are they? Has no one condemned you?" She said, "No one, sir." And Jesus said, "Neither do I condemn you. Go your way, and from now on do not sin again."

SPIRITUAL REFLECTION

I want to be ready. Be ready. Get ready. Pay attention to the things of God. Paying attention to the things of God puts the things that are not of God into sharp contrast. To be ready is to live in the world with a discerning heart, a heart that is open to choosing what is good, true, and beautiful. To be ready is to make a commitment to be like Jesus and to work like Jesus.

One of the most poignant expressions among African Americans these days is "woke." It connotes the opposite of ignorance. Woke, to describe a person, refers to one's alertness to injustice in society, especially racism. For one to be ready, one has to remain grounded in the awareness of the world and reality beyond oneself. The

Christian call from Jesus Christ and the prophets is all about being ready, and being ready always implies being awake.

This Spiritual mentions John. There is a strong possibility that John could mean John the Baptist, John the beloved disciple, or John the writer of the book of Revelations/the Apocalypse. John in the Christian tradition represents one who is called to prepare the way for Jesus, one who is called to love Jesus, and one who is called to reveal the activities of God in the world today. As Christians, without a doubt, we are called to be like John, because whichever John we see in the gospels is one who wants to be ready.

John the Baptist, as we know, was killed because of his witness to Jesus. He spoke truth to power and paid with his very life for speaking truth. His life continues to inspire us to remain faithful to the truth, even if we have to suffer for it. In the Christian community, we continue to celebrate his life as a life lived for Jesus, a life that pointed to Jesus in every way.

The Slaves sang about wanting to walk like John into Jerusalem. We call to mind the expression that encourages us to "walk the talk." Indeed, the John who walks into Jerusalem is the one who shows us what it means not just to talk about Jesus but to walk like Jesus into the city of Jerusalem. We keep in mind that Jerusalem is the city of peace and that in peace, there can be no cruelty and inhumane treatment of others.

John the beloved disciple is recorded in the gospels as being loved by Jesus. This is our goal, too: to be loved by Jesus. But being loved by Jesus is automatic, because we know that God created us in love, for love, and to be love. An important distinction of John, the beloved disciple, is that he remained at the foot of the cross with the Mother of Jesus. By remaining at the foot of the cross, he was given the task of taking care of the mother of Jesus, as if she were his own. When we remain at the cross, Jesus invites us into the ministry of caring for each other as family.

John, in the Book of Revelation, speaks about the inbreaking of God in the past, present, and future. We are invited by John to be witnesses of and for Christ yesterday, today, and tomorrow. In the midst of suffering and turmoil, we point to the presence of God by being witnesses to the God of Life.

"To walk in Jerusalem just like John" means to be responsive, to point the way to Jesus, to practice love in the world, and to be a prophetic voice for justice. John symbolizes a woke persona. He is ready. I want to be ready. Get ready.

SPIRITUAL COMMITMENT

- Reread the Spiritual. What do you need to be ready or woke?

- Jerusalem means the city of peace. Where do you see the need for peace in America today, especially in the area of race relations?

- How do these scriptures invite you to think differently about justice, bearing witness to Christ, or walking as a child of God?

- Imagine you are John the Baptist or the beloved disciple and write a letter of encouragement from that perspective to your family or church.

- Do you want to be ready? What exactly does that mean for you?

O, Freedom!

O, freedom! O, freedom! O, freedom,
Over me,
And before I'd be a slave,
I'll be buried in my grave,
And go home to my Lord and be free.

No more moaning. No more moaning.
    No more moaning,
Over me,
And before I'd be a slave,
I'll be buried in my grave,
And go home to my Lord and be free.

No more weeping. No more weeping.
    No more weeping,
Over me,
And before I'd be a slave,
I'll be buried in my grave,
And go home to my Lord and be free.

There'll be praying. There'll be praying.
    There'll be praying,
Over me,
And before I'd be a slave,
I'll be buried in my grave,
And go home to my Lord and be free.

SCRIPTURE
Philemon 1:8-22

For this reason, though I am bold enough in Christ to command you to do your duty, yet I would rather appeal to you on the basis of love—and I, Paul, do this as an old man, and now also as a prisoner of Christ Jesus. I am appealing to you for my child, Onesimus, whose father I have become during my imprisonment. Formerly he was useless to you, but now he is indeed useful both to you and to me. I am sending him, that is, my own heart, back to you. I wanted to keep him with me, so that he might be of service to me in your place during my imprisonment for the gospel; but I preferred to do nothing without your consent, in order that your good deed might be voluntary and not something forced. Perhaps this is the reason he was separated from you for a while, so that you might have him back forever, no longer as a slave but more than a slave, a beloved brother—especially to me but how much more to you, both in the flesh and in the Lord. So if you consider me your partner, welcome him as you would welcome me. If he has wronged you in any way, or owes you anything, charge that to my account. I, Paul, am writing this with my own hand: I will repay it. I say nothing about your owing me even your own self. Yes, brother, let me have this benefit from you in the Lord! Refresh my heart in Christ. Confident of your obedience, I am writing to you, knowing that you will do even more than I say. One thing more—prepare a guest room for me, for I am hoping through your prayers to be restored to you.

Psalm 103:6-7

The LORD executes righteousness and judgment for all who are oppressed. He made his ways known to Moses and his works to the children of Israel.

John 13:12-30

After he had washed their feet, had put on his robe, and had returned to the table, he said to them, "Do you know what I have done to you? You call me Teacher and Lord—and you are right, for that is what I am. So if I, your Lord and Teacher, have washed your feet, you also ought to wash one another's feet. For I have set you an example, that you also should do as I have done to you. Very truly, I tell you, servants are not greater than their master, nor are messengers greater than the one who sent them. If you know these things, you are blessed if you do them.

I am not speaking of all of you; I know whom I have chosen. But it is to fulfill the scripture, 'The one who ate my bread has lifted his heel against me.' I tell you this now, before it occurs, so that when it does occur, you may believe that I am he. Very truly, I tell you, whoever receives one whom I send receives me; and whoever receives me receives him who sent me." After saying this Jesus was troubled in spirit, and declared, "Very truly, I tell you, one of you will betray me." The disciples looked at one another, uncertain of whom he was speaking. One of his disciples—the one whom Jesus loved—was reclining next to him; Simon Peter therefore motioned to him to ask Jesus of whom he was speaking. So while reclining next to Jesus, he asked him, "Lord, who is it?" Jesus answered, "It is the one to whom I give this piece of bread when I have dipped it in the dish." So when he had dipped the piece of bread, he gave it to Judas son of Simon Iscariot. After he received the piece of bread, Satan entered into him. Jesus said to him, "Do quickly what you are going to do." Now no one at the table knew why he said this to him. Some thought that, because Judas had the common purse, Jesus was telling him, "Buy what we need for the festival;" or, that he should give something to the poor. So, after receiving the piece of bread, he immediately went out. And it was night.

SPIRITUAL REFLECTION

Slaves had one overarching desire: to be free. You could say that this desire for freedom is intrinsic for every human being. What the Slaves experienced for four centuries, no human being would have desired or wished to endure. How they yearned to be free. On the western shores of Africa, on the ships that brought them across the Atlantic Ocean, on the plantations throughout the newly colonized lands, and everywhere that there were Slaves, the burning desire was to be free. Some escaped. Others chose death over slavery.

O, freedom! O, freedom! O, freedom over me. And before I'd be a slave, I'll be buried in my grave, and go home to my Lord and be free. Harriet Tubman, born into slavery, escaped slavery and dedicated her life to liberating as many slaves as possible. Born in 1822, she devoted her life to this freedom work until her death in 1913. She was a religious woman, a devout Methodist, who strongly believed that God hated slavery and did not wish any human being to be enslaved. She was called Moses by those who admired her, and her bravery and mission were well known among the Slaves. The words of this Spiritual could have been her very words: *And before I'd be a slave, I'll be buried in my grave, and go home to my Lord and be free.*

The slave masters reserved the most demeaning and cruel acts for those Slaves who tried to run away or who helped to secure freedom for others. Even the horrific punishments meted out to the Slaves could not prevent brave men and women from seeking their freedom. They carried the light of hope deep within them and everyday pondered their liberation. They put their lives behind it.

It is noteworthy that there were many anti-slavery activists and abolitionists who worked along with many Slaves to overturn slavery and its laws. The life of Harriet Tubman invites us to think about what we might have done during the time of slavery. An escaped Slave herself, she made some fifteen missions to rescue approximately seventy-five enslaved people, including family and friends. Her tenacity invites us to think about what we are doing to combat the systemic racism in our day.

It is important for us to honor the ways the Slaves understood God and God's desire for their flourishing. Though they were enslaved, they knew that God wanted to preserve them from slavery, not just free them from sin. This Spiritual speaks volumes about what the Slaves knew about God's desire for them.

SPIRITUAL COMMITMENT

- Reread the Spiritual. How do you think about emotional, spiritual, and physical freedom?

- What do the scriptures have to say to you about your call to live in freedom?

- How might God be calling you to disrupt systemic injustice to become an agent of liberation?

- Think about places and situations today where people are enslaved and ways in which you can make a difference.

- What can you learn from the life of Harriet Tubman?

Ready

Better be ready, better be ready, better be ready,
Ready to try on your glory robe.

O, rise up children, get your crown,
And by our Savior's side sit down.

What a glorious morning that will be,
Our friends and Jesus, we shall see.

O shout you Christians, you're gaining ground.
We'll shout old Satan's kingdom down.

I soon shall reach that golden shore,
And sing the songs we sang before.

SCRIPTURE
James 2:14-26

What good is it, my brothers and sisters, if you say you have faith but do not have works? Can faith save you? If a brother or sister is naked and lacks daily food, and one of you says to them, "Go in peace; keep warm and eat your fill," and yet you do not supply their bodily needs, what is the good of that? So faith by itself, if it has no works, is dead. But someone will say, "You have faith and I have works." Show me your faith apart from your works, and I by my works will show you my faith. You believe that God is one; you do well. Even the demons believe—and shudder. Do you want to be shown, you senseless person, that faith apart from works is barren? Was not our ancestor Abraham justified by works when he offered his son Isaac on the altar? You see that faith was active along with his works, and faith was brought to completion by the works. Thus the scripture was fulfilled that says, "Abraham believed God, and it was reckoned to him as righteousness," and he was called the friend of God. You see that a person is justified by works and not by faith alone. Likewise, was not Rahab the prostitute also justified by works when she welcomed the messengers and sent them out by another road? For just as the body without the spirit is dead, so faith without works is also dead.

Psalm 127:1-3

Unless the LORD builds the house, their labor is in vain who build it. Unless the LORD watches over the city, in vain the watchman keeps his vigil. It is in vain that you rise so early and go to bed so late; vain, too, to eat the bread of toil, for he gives to his beloved sleep.

John 17:6-19

"I have made your name known to those whom you gave me from the world. They were yours, and you gave them to me, and they have kept your word. Now they know that everything you have given me is from you; for the words that you gave to me I have given to them, and they have received them and know in truth that I came from you; and they have believed that you sent me. I am asking on their behalf; I am not asking on behalf of the world, but on behalf of those whom you gave me, because they are yours. All mine are yours, and yours are mine; and I have been glorified in them.

And now I am no longer in the world, but they are in the world, and I am coming to you. Holy Father, protect them in your name that you have given me, so that they may be one, as we are one. While I was with them, I protected them in your name that you have given me. I guarded them, and not one of them was lost except the one destined to be lost, so that the scripture might be fulfilled. But now I am coming to you, and I speak these things in the world so that they may have my joy made complete in themselves. I have given them your word, and the world has hated them because they do not belong to the world, just as I do not belong to the world. I am not asking you to take them out of the world, but I ask you to protect them from the evil one. They do not belong to the world, just as I do not belong to the world.

Sanctify them in the truth; your word is truth. As you have sent me into the world, so I have sent them into the world. And for their sakes I sanctify myself, so that they also may be sanctified in truth.

SPIRITUAL REFLECTION

O, rise up children, get your crown, and by our Savior's side sit down. The word children in this line of the Spiritual reminds me of the children involved in the Civil Rights movement.

In the early months of 1963, Dr. Martin Luther King Jr. and other leaders in Alabama recognized that interest in the Civil Rights movement was waning, and many adults were unwilling to participate in the activities of the movement. Fewer people attended the sit-ins, the boycotts, and the marches. As more and more of the leaders were jailed and it became clear that few changes in desegregation were underway, it was hard to inspire adults to participate in the movement.

One of the leaders suggested that the movement reach out to the teenagers in the high schools. Of course, there was a practical reason for this: adults would lose their jobs for joining the protests; high schoolers, for the most part, had no jobs to lose.

Dr. King was opposed to having children involved at first, but he always encouraged the other leaders to implement their ideas, so he was willing to see how this would work. On May 2, 1963, more than 1,000 students ages 7-18 marched with signs and sang Spirituals. Many of the children were arrested as they marched to City Hall and to lunch counters.

Children being arrested and harassed by the police made the TV evening news across the country. Eventually, nearly 3,000 children were arrested as more and more children joined the marches and protest. It seemed that the witness of the children inspired the adults. Many people, including Dr. King, believed that the children who rose up saved the Civil Rights movement. In the words of the Spiritual, the children rose up, got their crown, and sat down by their Savior's side. *O, rise up children, get your crown, and by our Savior's side sit down.*

The Slaves who sang this Spiritual affirmed their faith in God and reminded each other to be ready. Again, the term ready in the Christian tradition has always been a call to action, a call to live righteous lives, and a call to confront the evils of the day. For the Slaves, to have faith was to put one's faith in action. *O shout you Christians, you're gaining ground. We'll shout old Satan's kingdom down. I soon shall reach that golden shore, and sing the songs we sang before.*

SPIRITUAL COMMITMENT

- Reread the Spiritual. What does it mean for you to be ready to put your faith into action?

- Spend some time reflecting on how your views on racism have changed or been challenged since your childhood.

- How do these scriptures invite you to examine your ongoing commitment to God and the issues of social justice?

- Life is all about adapting and taking risks in order to grow. How is God calling you to deepen your Christian commitments by adapting and taking risks?

- When has a child shown you an important truth or led the way in showing Christ's love?

Monument

Black and
Beautiful
Uprising from the
Beginning, proclaiming this ever-
Ancient ever-new reality
While we were at supper
And during the blessing
This is my body
This is my blood
Remember the black
Ethiopian dust that flew
To the shores of Ghana
Like hands outstretched from
Sea to shining sea fighting
against the System
that tries to justify
trying to sell our soul—
We survive and rise
We will not celebrate
Hate, oppression, and lies
Our beautiful and Black
Ancestors told the Ashanti truth:
We never start a war
But we will fight until
The end.
We know we shall
Win. We are confident in the victory
of good over stupid,
And ugly,
And evil.
Matter.

Key Man Lock the Door and Gone

A pair of every animal
Was saved in the ark,
Saved in the ark,
Saved in ark.

A pair of every animal
Was saved in the ark.
Key man lock the door and gone.

Key man, key man, key man, key man.
Key man lock the door and gone,
Key man, key man, key man, key man.
Key man lock the door and gone.

SCRIPTURE

1 Peter 1:3-12

Blessed be the God and Father of our Lord Jesus Christ! By his great mercy he has given us a new birth into a living hope through the resurrection of Jesus Christ from the dead, and into an inheritance that is imperishable, undefiled, and unfading, kept in heaven for you, who are being protected by the power of God through faith for a salvation ready to be revealed in the last time.

In this you rejoice, even if now for a little while you have had to suffer various trials, so that the genuineness of your faith—being more precious than gold that, though perishable, is tested by fire—may be found to result in praise and glory and honor when Jesus Christ is revealed. Although you have not seen him, you love him; and even though you do not see him now, you believe in him and rejoice with an indescribable and glorious joy, for you are receiving the outcome of your faith, the salvation of your souls.

Concerning this salvation, the prophets who prophesied of the grace that was to be yours made careful search and inquiry, inquiring about the person or time that the Spirit of Christ within them indicated when it testified in advance to the sufferings destined for Christ and the subsequent glory. It was revealed to them that they were serving not themselves but you, in regard to the things that have now been announced to you through those who brought you good news by the Holy Spirit sent from heaven—things into which angels long to look!

Psalm 130:1,4-5

Out of the depths have I called to you, O LORD; LORD, hear my voice; let your ears consider well the voice of my supplication....I wait for the LORD; my soul waits for him; in his word is my hope. My soul waits for the LORD, more than watchmen for the morning, more than watchmen for the morning.

John 19:16b-30

So they took Jesus; and carrying the cross by himself, he went out to what is called The Place of the Skull, which in Hebrew is called Golgotha. There they crucified him, and with him two others, one on either side, with Jesus between them.

Pilate also had an inscription written and put on the cross. It read, "Jesus of Nazareth, the King of the Jews." Many of the Jews read this inscription, because the place where Jesus was crucified was near the city; and it was written in Hebrew, in Latin, and in Greek. Then the chief priests of the Jews said to Pilate, "Do not write, 'The King of the Jews,' but, 'This man said, I am King of the Jews.'" Pilate answered, "What I have written I have written." When the soldiers had crucified Jesus, they took his clothes and divided them into four parts, one for each soldier. They also took his tunic; now the tunic was seamless, woven in one piece from the top. So they said to one another, "Let us not tear it, but cast lots for it to see who will get it." This was to fulfill what the scripture says, "They divided my clothes among themselves, and for my clothing they cast lots." And that is what the soldiers did. Meanwhile, standing near the cross of Jesus were his mother, and his mother's sister, Mary the wife of Clopas, and Mary Magdalene. When Jesus saw his mother and the disciple whom he loved standing beside her, he said to his mother, "Woman, here is your son." Then he said to the disciple, "Here is your mother." And from that hour the disciple took her into his own home. After this, when Jesus knew that all was now finished, he said (in order to fulfill the scripture), "I am thirsty." A jar full of sour wine was standing there. So they put a sponge full of the wine on a branch of hyssop and held it to his mouth. When Jesus had received the wine, he said, "It is finished." Then he bowed his head and gave up his spirit.

SPIRITUAL REFLECTION

We are all connected, all children of God, and we are a part of all that exists and happens in the world. In this Spiritual about animals, the ark, and the key man, we get a glimpse once again into the complex ideas celebrated in simple lyrics.

"A pair of every animal" speaks to the attention that God gave to everything. Noah warned the people of his day that God would destroy the earth if they did not repent and turn away from their sins. Of course, they did not listen. Readers of the story of Noah sometimes miss the most important element of the story. The writer of the story was more interested in pointing to a man and his family who listened to God, even though to many, the wishes and demands of God seemed bizarre. Imagine God telling you that a flood was coming and that you needed to build an ark and collect a pair of every animal to live with you and your family while the earth was flooded.

Noah listened. Noah believed. Noah did what the Lord commanded. The ark is evidence that Noah remained faithful to God, did the hard things, did the things that cost a lot, and did the things that made people mock him.

This Spiritual is an affirmation of the faith of Noah. Slavery was evidence of what happens when people do not listen to God. The Slaves knew the story, and they knew that those who do not heed God receive God's condemnation.

Because Noah listened, life survived upon the earth. Because the Slaves listened and believed in God, they had hope for survival in this life and the next. The Slaves believed that God would never abandon them and they listened faithfully.

*Key man lock the door and gone. Key man, key man, key man, key man. Key man lock the door and gon*e. Yes, there will be a reckoning, and in the reckoning is the fulfillment of God's word and God's vindication. The key man is God, and the locking of the door is the fulfillment of what God promised Noah.

SPIRITUAL COMMITMENT

- Reread the Spiritual. How do you listen to the voice of God?

- What is the ark in your life?

- Spend some time reflecting on how all rights are related.

- How do you participate in the care of our planet and the animals entrusted to our care?

- Spend some time rereading the scriptures. Pray for the grace to listen more deeply to God, in light of the African American experience of faith and injustice.

O Bye and Bye,
Bye and Bye

O bye and bye, bye and bye
I'm going to lay down my heavy load.

I know my robe's gonna fit me well.
I'm gonna lay down my heavy load.
I tried it on at the gates of hell.
I'm going to lay down my heavy load.

O hell is deep and in dark despair,
I'm gonna lay down my heavy load.
So stop, po' sinner and don't despair.
I'm gonna lay down my heavy load.

O, Christian, can't you arise and tell,
I'm gonna lay down my heavy load.
That Jesus did do all things well.
I'm gonna to lay down my heavy load.

SCRIPTURE

1 John 4:7-21

Beloved, let us love one another, because love is from God; everyone who loves is born of God and knows God. Whoever does not love does not know God, for God is love. God's love was revealed among us in this way: God sent his only Son into the world so that we might live through him. In this is love, not that we loved God but that he loved us and sent his Son to be the atoning sacrifice for our sins. Beloved, since God loved us so much, we also ought to love one another. No one has ever seen God; if we love one another, God lives in us, and his love is perfected in us. By this we know that we abide in him and he in us, because he has given us of his Spirit.

And we have seen and do testify that the Father has sent his Son as the Savior of the world. God abides in those who confess that Jesus is the Son of God, and they abide in God. So we have known and believe the love that God has for us. God is love, and those who abide in love abide in God, and God abides in them.

Love has been perfected among us in this: that we may have boldness on the day of judgment, because as he is, so are we in this world. There is no fear in love, but perfect love casts out fear; for fear has to do with punishment, and whoever fears has not reached perfection in love. We love because he first loved us. Those who say, "I love God," and hate their brothers or sisters, are liars; for those who do not love a brother or sister whom they have seen, cannot love God whom they have not seen. The commandment we have from him is this: those who love God must love their brothers and sisters also.

Psalm 139:1-2

LORD, you have searched me out and known me; you know my sitting down and my rising up; you discern my thoughts from afar. You trace my journeys and my resting-places and are acquainted with all my ways.

John 20:1-10

Early on the first day of the week, while it was still dark, Mary Magdalene came to the tomb and saw that the stone had been removed from the tomb. So she ran and went to Simon Peter and the other disciple, the one whom Jesus loved, and said to them, "They have taken the Lord out of the tomb, and we do not know where they have laid him." Then Peter and the other disciple set out and went toward the tomb. The two were running together, but the other disciple outran Peter and reached the tomb first.

He bent down to look in and saw the linen wrappings lying there, but he did not go in. Then Simon Peter came, following him, and went into the tomb. He saw the linen wrappings lying there, and the cloth that had been on Jesus's head, not lying with the linen wrappings but rolled up in a place by itself. Then the other disciple, who reached the tomb first, also went in, and he saw and believed; for as yet they did not understand the scripture, that he must rise from the dead. Then the disciples returned to their homes.

SPIRITUAL REFLECTION

I'm gonna lay down my heavy load. O, Christian, can't you arise and tell. I'm gonna lay down my heavy load. That Jesus did do all things well. I'm gonna lay down my heavy load. When the Slaves sang about the realities of their lives, it was with a sad and profound acknowledgement that they had a heavy and inhumane burden to bear. Again, it is noteworthy that the Slaves saw Jesus not as a disinterested onlooker but as one who suffered like them and with them. In Jesus, they experienced God calling them to remain true to their faith, themselves, and each other.

One of the most shocking realities to accept is that the church largely supported and benefited from slavery. People used the Bible to justify and perpetrate grave sins against the African peoples. God's word of sacrificial love, forgiveness, love of neighbor, and welcome of the stranger were deliberately misinterpreted and falsely taught in order to maintain the system of slavery. Christian colonizers, slave traders, and plantation owners chose to consciously deny the teachings, in order to attempt these sinful contradictions and begin to normalize them. How does one square love of God and neighbor with the dehumanizing hatred and oppression of the Slaves?

Even after the end of slavery, churches continued to support racist teachings and interpretation of scriptures. Many religious leaders preached segregation and encouraged their congregants to treat African Americans as less than human. Sadly, the churches were some of the greatest defenders and upholders of racism. Mainline congregations encouraged the founding of congregations exclusively for African Americans as a means of ensuring there was no integration.

It is important to remember that the slave masters too, preached a scripture that supported and propped up the tenets of slavery. But the religious leaders among the Slaves did not buy into what the slave masters told them about God. They knew and experienced a God of love and freedom. Yet, they realized they had to be careful in how they preached about God's desire for their freedom, so they often used Spirituals as a way to spread the message without incurring the wrath. The Spirituals, taken together, form a constellation that speaks to a nuanced and sophisticated understanding of God. They reveal that the Slaves understood they were loved by God, made in the very image and likeness of God, and were accompanied by God at every step.

At the beginning of the twentieth century, an awakening to matters of justice and equality led to an increase in the churches' posture against racism and the ongoing dehumanization of African Americans. In the 1950's, inter-faith religious leaders from across the United States participated in the Civil Rights movement; their presence helped to redeem the role of the churches in slavery and the ongoing experience of racism.

Today, many Christians are still unapologetically racist or segregationist. Thankfully, this is not a majority, but it does call us to live in such a way that the love and justice of God is promoted for all oppressed people.

SPIRITUAL COMMITMENT

- Reread the Spiritual. How is God calling you to respond to the suffering of others?

- Spend some time reading Dr. Martin Luther King's Jr.'s "I have a dream" speech.

- How are the scripture readings calling you, your church, and the American society to act differently?

- Can a Christian be racist?

- What do the Spirituals and the scriptures for today have to teach us about a Christian response to the Black Lives Matter movement?

Never Get Weary Yet

I never get weary yet.
I never get weary yet.
I've been down in the valley
A very long time,
But I never get weary yet.

We never get weary yet.
We never get weary yet.
We've been down in the valley
A very long time,
But we never get weary yet.

I am walking on to Mt. Zion.
I am walking on to Mt. Zion.
We've been down in the valley
A very long time,
But we never get weary yet.

SCRIPTURE
Revelation 3:14-22

"And to the angel of the church in Laodicea write: The words of the Amen, the faithful and true witness, the origin of God's creation: "I know your works; you are neither cold nor hot. I wish that you were either cold or hot. So, because you are lukewarm, and neither cold nor hot, I am about to spit you out of my mouth. For you say, 'I am rich, I have prospered, and I need nothing.' You do not realize that you are wretched, pitiable, poor, blind, and naked. Therefore I counsel you to buy from me gold refined by fire so that you may be rich; and white robes to clothe you and to keep the shame of your nakedness from being seen; and salve to anoint your eyes so that you may see. I reprove and discipline those whom I love. Be earnest, therefore, and repent. Listen! I am standing at the door, knocking; if you hear my voice and open the door, I will come in to you and eat with you, and you with me. To the one who conquers I will give a place with me on my throne, just as I myself conquered and sat down with my Father on his throne. Let anyone who has an ear listen to what the Spirit is saying to the churches."

Psalm 146:7-8

The LORD sets the prisoners free; the LORD opens the eyes of the blind; the LORD lifts up those who are bowed down; The LORD loves the righteous; the LORD cares for the stranger; he sustains the orphan and widow, but frustrates the way of the wicked.

John 20:11-18

But Mary stood weeping outside the tomb. As she wept, she bent over to look into the tomb; and she saw two angels in white, sitting where the body of Jesus had been lying, one at the head and the other at the feet. They said to her, "Woman, why are you weeping?" She said to them, "They have taken away my Lord, and I do not know where they have laid him." When she had said this, she turned around and saw Jesus standing there, but she did not know that it was Jesus. Jesus said to her, "Woman, why are you weeping? Whom are you looking for?" Supposing him to be the gardener, she said to him, "Sir, if you have carried him away, tell me where you have laid him, and I will take him away." Jesus said to her, "Mary!" She turned and said to him in Hebrew, "*Rabbouni!*" (which means Teacher). Jesus said to her, "Do not hold on to me, because I have not yet ascended to the Father. But go to my brothers and say to them, 'I am ascending to my Father and your Father, to my God and your God.' " Mary Magdalene went and announced to the disciples, "I have seen the Lord;" and she told them that he had said these things to her.

SPIRITUAL REFLECTION

I never get weary yet. I never get weary yet. I've been down in the valley a very long time, but I never get weary yet. Life, by its very nature, has moments of intense suffering and pain; some experience this reality on a daily basis. When we examine the life of Jesus, we see demonstrated the care and compassion of God. God notices our burdens, our suffering, our pain, and all that makes our lives challenging. In truth, the God we meet in Jesus Christ is the God who suffers with us: the God of compassion, Immanuel, who journeys with us.

When you experience pain and suffering in your own life, what gives you strength to go on and keep believing? Guarding your strength is an important aspect of the spiritual life. Indeed, the faithfulness to which we are called is one that requires that we remain attentive, alert, and open to the presence of God, especially when we suffer and experience pain.

For the Slaves who encountered God, God's message through Christ was not lost on them. They recognized that Christ invited the "weary and heavy laden" to come to God. In this Spiritual, the Slaves affirmed their unwavering hope in God. The Slaves proclaimed that they have been "down in the valley a very long time," but they will not get weary, because God is with them. One wonders if Psalm 23 was a special psalm for them. The psalmist writes that even though they may pass through the valley of darkness, they would fear no evil. Knowing that God is with us in our suffering and pain makes all the difference. It helps to keep the weariness at bay.

Those of us who have faced suffering, pain, trauma, and death know that the experiences have a way of showing up, reappearing at different stages in our lives. This Spiritual sung by the Slaves reminds us that the suffering and pain experienced in slavery still continues today. Four hundred years of oppression and cruelty marked the experiences of the Slaves and still reverberates in today's reality. Think for a moment of the experience of African

Americans during the beginning of the twentieth century and the experience of segregation and Jim Crow. Think of the pain and suffering experienced by African Americans as they demanded their rights in the 1950's, 60's, and 70's. Think of the determination they had as they faced racist politicians, church leaders, fire hoses, dogs, and hostile fellow Americans. It takes a lot of courage and faith not to get weary.

In today's American society, the suffering and pain of slavery live on and rise to the surface in many ways. African Americans face both overt and subtle forms of daily discrimination, prejudice, and racism. African Americans are still being killed by the police who are not held accountable; they are still being killed because of poverty. The trauma from slavery and the continued trauma from systemic racism is real and requires all our attention as a society. All of us can play a part in ensuring that our African American brothers and sisters do not get weary, and that our African American brothers and sisters know that we join in the work for healing, reconciliation, and justice.

SPIRITUAL COMMITMENT

- Reread the Spiritual. How might God be calling you to stay strong in facing the systemic racism in America?

- What do the scriptures for the day teach us about persevering in our call to be God's healing presence in a broken world?

- Spend some time thinking of the moments in your life when you experienced pain and suffering or racialized trauma.

- Make a list of the ways you think African Americans continue to suffer in this country.

- How and where do your compassion and faith confront the sin of racism and its ongoing effects?

I Want Jesus to Walk with Me

I want Jesus to walk with me.
I want Jesus to walk with me.
All along my pilgrim journey,
I want Jesus to walk with me.

In my trials, Lord walk with me.
In my trials, Lord walk with me.
When the shades of life are falling,
I want Jesus to walk with me.

In my sorrows, Lord, walk with me.
In my sorrow, Lord walk with me.
When my heart within is aching,
I want Jesus to walk with me.
I want Jesus to walk with me.

SCRIPTURE
Revelation 21:1-8

Then I saw a new heaven and a new earth; for the first heaven and the first earth had passed away, and the sea was no more. And I saw the holy city, the new Jerusalem, coming down out of heaven from God, prepared as a bride adorned for her husband. And I heard a loud voice from the throne saying, "See, the home of God is among mortals. He will dwell with them as their God; they will be his peoples, and God himself will be with them; he will wipe every tear from their eyes. Death will be no more; mourning and crying and pain will be no more, for the first things have passed away." And the one who was seated on the throne said, "See, I am making all things new." Also he said, "Write this, for these words are trustworthy and true." Then he said to me, "It is done! I am the Alpha and the Omega, the beginning and the end. To the thirsty I will give water as a gift from the spring of the water of life. Those who conquer will inherit these things, and I will be their God and they will be my children. But as for the cowardly, the faithless, the polluted, the murderers, the fornicators, the sorcerers, the idolaters, and all liars, their place will be in the lake that burns with fire and sulfur, which is the second death."

Psalm 150:1-3

Hallelujah! Praise God in his holy temple; praise him in the firmament of his power. Praise him for his mighty acts; praise him for his excellent greatness. Praise him with the blast of the ram's-horn; praise him with lyre and harp.

John 20:19-31

When it was evening on that day, the first day of the week, and the doors of the house where the disciples had met were locked for fear of the Jews, Jesus came and stood among them and said, "Peace be with you." After he said this, he showed them his hands and his side. Then the disciples rejoiced when they saw the Lord. Jesus said to them again, "Peace be with you. As the Father has sent me, so I send you." When he had said this, he breathed on them and said to them, "Receive the Holy Spirit. If you forgive the sins of any, they are forgiven them; if you retain the sins of any, they are retained." But Thomas (who was called the Twin), one of the twelve, was not with them when Jesus came. So the other disciples told him, "We have seen the Lord." But he said to them, "Unless I see the mark of the nails in his hands, and put my finger in the mark of the nails and my hand in his side, I will not believe."

A week later his disciples were again in the house, and Thomas was with them. Although the doors were shut, Jesus came and stood among them and said, "Peace be with you." Then he said to

Thomas, "Put your finger here and see my hands. Reach out your hand and put it in my side. Do not doubt but believe." Thomas answered him, "My Lord and my God!" Jesus said to him, "Have you believed because you have seen me? Blessed are those who have not seen and yet have come to believe." Now Jesus did many other signs in the presence of his disciples, which are not written in this book. But these are written so that you may come to believe that Jesus is the Messiah, the Son of God, and that through believing you may have life in his name.

SPIRITUAL REFLECTION

I want Jesus to walk with me. I want Jesus to walk with me. All along my pilgrim journey, I want Jesus to walk with me.

This, indeed, is the most important prayer along the Christian journey. At the foundation of discipleship is our desire for Jesus to walk with us. To desire Jesus to walk with us is to invite Jesus into every aspect of our lives.

The term walk, from the time of slavery and presently in the African American community, refers to deep commitment and integrity as one walks in the world. It is used in the phrase, "Don't just talk the talk; walk the walk." For Jesus to walk with us daily requires that we live a life that is always open to Jesus, a life that welcomes Jesus, and recognizes the sovereignty of Jesus in our lives. This is the source of our integrity.

The Slaves who sang this hymn knew a lot about the life of Jesus. As they read and heard the scriptures, they noticed whom Jesus walked with and what happened as Jesus walked along. They noticed where Jesus went and the healing that happened as he walked along. They noticed whom Jesus called as he walked along the Sea of Galilee. They noticed that, as he walked, he brought good news to the poor, set prisoners free, cured the lame, brought sight to the blind, and proclaimed rest for the downtrodden. When the Slaves saw all that happened as Jesus walked throughout his life on earth; they wanted Jesus to walk with them.

In my trials, Lord walk with me. In my trials, Lord walk with me. When the shades of life are falling, I want Jesus to walk with me.

When the Slaves sang that they wanted Jesus to walk with them in their trials, they were offering the most profound profession of their faith. Knowing the trial of Jesus and how he was mocked, dehumanized, beaten, crucified, and eventually killed gave the Slaves the comfort of accompaniment. Jesus understood. Jesus was walking with them. In truth, when we can call on someone to walk with us in the difficult moments, we know we have a friend.

Imagine the faith of the Slaves, who knew that in their trial, God was walking with them. The Spirituals demonstrate the faith of the Slaves, and this Spiritual, in particular, expresses that faith in a deep and poignant way. Imagine what the slave masters must have thought as they heard the Slaves singing this Spiritual. Let there be no doubt: this, indeed, is the lived spirituality of many African Americans and people who suffer.

In my sorrows, Lord, walk with me. In my sorrow, Lord walk with me. When my heart within is aching, I want Jesus to walk with me. I want Jesus to walk with me.

When Americans witnessed the suffering of the demonstrators marching throughout the South for their civil rights, their attitude toward segregation and Jim Crow changed. In present-day America, the sorrows witnessed as police shot or killed African Americans have led to a national outcry for justice and peace. Sorrow formed part of the reality of the Slaves, and there was no one to help them or show them mercy. But through their faith, they knew that Jesus would not abandon them in their sorrow, and they knew Jesus walked with them. In their sorrow, they understood the sorrow of Jesus. And what they came to know about the sorrows of Jesus gave them the strength and courage to persevere. In our own age, Jesus is near to the broken-hearted, too. The Christian life calls us to put our faith in action and walk with those who suffer and experience racism today.

SPIRITUAL COMMITMENT

- Reread the Spiritual. What does it mean for you to invite Jesus to walk with you in your challenging moments?

- What does it mean to walk the walk of the Christian life, especially as it relates to loving your neighbor?

- Who has walked with you in your trials? How have you walked with others who have experienced difficulties?

- How do the scriptures invite you to walk with others and to respond to social injustice?

- If you were to write a letter to a Slave community, what would you write?

- How will you join with communities committed to the fight for justice? What is your deepest intention with regard to upending prejudice, discrimination, and racial hatreds in this country?

Endure

My mother always says
She even said it yesterday
What you can't cure
you must endure.
John Brown's body lies
A stinking in the grave
But his truth is marching on
That is who the soul rebel is who controls the
Past and controls the future and endures
The present
Trodding down daily white supremacy and
Black subordination
Resisting the system
Psychic violence
Psychological exile
Come celebrate this marking, claiming
This proclaiming
This cure of the sickness in the
Story
(Yes, Mommy)
Enduring.

ACKNOWLEDGMENTS

The Spirituals remind me of the enduring faith of the Slaves. These songs of resilience, courage, faith, and freedom do three powerful things: they name the pain, face the reality, and claim the Way of Love. Now, that is true prayer; and we can all learn to pray more intently as we sing and pray these Spirituals.

These Spirituals help us repent, name the evils of racism, and commit to living our prayer and faith in such a way that we respect the dignity of every human being.

Thanks to Rachel Jones, Miriam McKenney, and Richelle Thompson of Forward Movement. I am especially indebted to Richelle for her wisdom, faith, commitment to social justice, and editorial skills. Thanks to the Rev. Dr. Kathy Bozzuti-Jones who was my chief sounding board. I cannot sing her praises and thank her enough.

The year 2020 was a challenging year. The pandemic ravaged families in America. Police brutality and the disregard for Black lives show us that we have a lot to do as a country in addressing the sins of racism. It was a year of singing the Spirituals.

The Black Lives Matter movement provided a "spiritual" chorus line for me as I wrote. One could say, the Spirituals proclaim that Black lives matter.

I want to thank the many women and men who have spoken out on behalf of racial justice and to those who have laid down their lives in the cause for racial justice. I offer a special thanks to Presiding Bishop Michael Curry who keeps calling us to "the path of love and the Way of Love."

I want to acknowledge that the fight against racial injustice continues. Hopefully, this book and the ongoing commitment we all can make to name the pain, face the reality, and claim the Way of Love will help us to "overcome" the racism in our society.

To sing and pray these Spirituals is to commit to justice and to respect the dignity of every human being.

God bless you and bless us all as we reflect on the Spirituals and Justice. Keep singing. Keep praying. We shall overcome.

ABOUT THE AUTHOR

The Rev. Dr. Mark Francisco Bozzuti-Jones is an Episcopal Jamaican priest at Trinity Church Wall Street in New York City. He is the priest and director of spiritual formation at Trinity's Retreat Center in West Cornwall, Connecticut.

A former Jesuit priest, Mark has missionary experience in Belize, Brazil, and Guyana. He believes that prayer, silence, and rest deepen our connection to God and allow us to name the pain, face the realities of our time, and claim the Way of Love.

He is an avid reader, award-winning author, and speaker, and has taught at elementary and university levels. He has a passion for the cultures in Latin America and the Caribbean.

His intellectual interests include the impact of social issues on faith and spirituality, racism, and plight of the poor. He loves flowers and Brazilian and Reggae music and believes in the inculturation of religion.

He is a frequent contributor at Forward Movement. His other books include *God Created*, *Jesus the Word*, *The Gospel of Barack Hussein Obama According to Mark* and *The Rastafari Book of Common Prayer*.

He is married to the Rev. Dr. Kathy Bozzuti-Jones; Mark Anthony is their son, the Negus.

ABOUT FORWARD MOVEMENT

Forward Movement is committed to inspiring disciples and empowering evangelists. Our ministry is lived out by creating resources such as books, small-group studies, apps, and conferences.

Our daily devotional, *Forward Day by Day*, is also available in Spanish (*Adelante Día a Día*) and Braille, online, as a podcast, and as an app for smartphones or tablets. It is mailed to more than fifty countries, and we donate nearly tens of thousands of copies each quarter to prisons, hospitals, and nursing homes.

We actively seek partners across the church and look for ways to provide resources that inspire and challenge. A ministry of the Episcopal Church for more than eighty years, Forward Movement is a nonprofit organization funded by sales of resources and by gifts from generous donors.

To learn more about Forward Movement and our resources, visit ForwardMovement.org. We are delighted to be doing this work and invite your prayers and support.